# EFFECTIVE COMMUNICATION FOR LAWYERS

## Presenting, Counseling, Persuading

**Michael P. Maslanka**
*UNT Dallas College of Law*

**Katherine Silver Kelly**
*The Ohio State Michael E. Moritz College of Law*

**Nicole T. LeBoeuf**
*Hallett & Perrin, P.C.*

WEST ACADEMIC

860 Blue Gentian Road, Suite 350
Eagan, MN 55121
1-877-888-1330



Published in the United States of America

**ISBN:** 979-8-89209-732-1

*For Julia Santos.*
*—Professor Michael P. Maslanka*

*For my parents, David and Dorothy Silver.*
*—Professor Katherine Silver Kelly*

*For my Dad, Herve J. LeBoeuf III, whose love of learning inspires me.*
*—Nicole T. LeBoeuf*

# Why Read This Book?

As a lawyer, you are required to give presentations, find and counsel clients, persuade audiences/juries, resolve disputes, brief partners, and much more.

Here is a truth: your legal education likely gave you little to no guidance on tackling these types of challenges.

But this truth is counterbalanced by another truth: these disparate tasks share a common throughline—the need to communicate effectively. Indeed, in some ways, you are not lawyers who are also communicators, you are communicators who also happen to be lawyers.

So, we wrote this book as a mentoring guide in three key areas: Presenting, Counseling, Persuading. It is intended as a starting point in developing your own styles as presenters, counselors, persuaders. While we have infused much of our advice from our experiences, our aspiration is helping you grow into the very best versions of yourself! To that end, we assembled a Board of Advisors, consisting of law students and new lawyers, for their input into the communication challenges faced by the readers of this book.

We hope you find nuggets of actionable advice for your future or ongoing practice; a starting place for discussions with your "three dimensional" mentors and colleagues; and a handy and friendly source of counsel and advice.

# HOW DO I USE THIS BOOK?

The book's structure is a function of these goals. It can be read cover to cover or consulted as needed. Access your communication "Challenges" by scanning the Table of Contents. Read the "Tools" suggested to meet them. Solidify these lessons via "By Way of Illustration" and "The Spotlight." From time to time, we provide experiential exercises to help you Find Your Voice. Here is a rundown of these elements:

- "The Challenge"

Questions you will ask yourselves in Presenting, Counseling, and Persuading such as "How Do I Start Drafting an Opening Statement?"; "How Do I Handle Tough Client Conversations?"; "How Do I Sustain Audience Engagement?"

- "Tools"

Following every Challenge is a variety of Tools to meet that Challenge. Some tools might work for you; others, perhaps not. Again, it is *your* toolbelt—assembled in a way that works best for you and your needs.

- "Tell and Show"

We did not want the book to be all Tell, no Show. Or as they say in Texas—all hat, no cattle. So here we explain the nature of the tools and how to use them. We often rely upon cognitive and psychological research. Effective communication is twisted together like a pretzel of science and human nature.

- "Finding Your Voice"

Professors Maslanka and LeBoeuf teach at the National Institute for Trial Advocacy (NITA). There they learned that one way of learning is by doing. This section focuses not on abstract exercises, but rather on tasks and assignments you face in practice. It is an opportunity to apply the knowledge that you've gained from the Challenges and corresponding Tools.

- "By Way of Illustration"

These were selected for their value as illustrations of the tools, for their role model value, and for their historical perspective.

- "The Spotlight"

Here, we focus on communication lessons learned from professional speakers, lawyers, and historical figures. Their lessons are ones often learned from the trial and the error of practice and the rough and tumble of life.

- "The Neurodiversity Insight"

Our thanks to co-author Professor Kelly whose many contributions to this book include educating us all (including her co-authors) on "neurodiversity." She writes and speaks on this topic as a nationally recognized expert in this area. She teaches that neurodiversity refers to the neurological variations in our brains. In short, people experience and interact in the world in many disparate ways.

Here are a few helpful definitions as you read these sections. Neurotypical describes a person whose neurological functions align with what is considered "standard." By contrast, neurodivergent is a nonmedical term defining individuals with differences in brain functions and behavioral traits compared to the neurotypical. As a non-medical term, it is not a condition that is diagnosed but rather an umbrella term for multiple conditions: ADHD, Autism Spectrum Disorder, Obsessive Compulsive Disorder, Tourette's Syndrome, Dysgraphia, Dyscalculia, Dyslexia, Dyspraxia, and more.

For all of us, lawyers and law students, the neurotypical and the neurodivergent, educators and students alike, a parting thought: the root word of "communicate" is "communis." Translation? "To share with others," which precisely describes what you will do in your life and career—with your knowledge, with your counsel, with your advocacy.

Let's commune!

Professor Michael P. Maslanka
Dallas, Texas

Professor Katherine Silver Kelly
Columbus, Ohio

Adjunct Professor Nicole T. LeBoeuf
Dallas, Texas

# ACKNOWLEDGMENTS

While books are often written solo (or, as here, by a trio), they can only be birthed from a multitude. My gratitude to Graduate Research Assistants Madelyn Morris and Julia Santos (now sister lawyers) for their commitment to this project. Julia also deserves credit for our book's uniquely user -friendly format. A debt is owed Professor Kelly for educating me on the communication challenges of the neurodiverse. I am further indebted to Professor LeBoeuf for schooling me on a variety of effective counseling and persuading techniques. Among the multitude are high school intern Rithya Cheela who was spot on with her research; Louis Higgins and Danny Buteyn at West Academic who were wonderful collaborators; and my friends and drivers Sebagadis Taddesa and Amarjitpal Gill who were—and continue to be—an indispensable part of my daily life.

Finally, my gratitude to Toussaint Downtown Brasserie for allowing me to camp out at my table during the brainstorming and writing of this book.

—Professor Michael P. Maslanka

What an honor it was to be invited into this incredible group of individuals, I could not have asked for better thought partners. The seemingly limitless depth and breadth of Professors Maslanka and LeBoeuf's experience and expertise is astounding. Thank you to the folks at West Academic for supporting and encouraging our sometimes-unconventional ideas; and my home institution, The Ohio State University Moritz College of Law, for providing scholarship support.

—Professor Katherine Silver Kelly

My work on this book in no small part honors and recalls the lessons taught by the late Dale C. Howe, my first leadership coach, who both mentored me and encouraged me to write, present, and teach.

My gratitude also goes to Julia Santos, who consistently gave excellent input (and encouraged me to meet deadlines). I am grateful to her and to my other colleagues at LeBoeuf Law,

PLLC, whose good work for our shared clients makes it possible for me to teach, write, and mentor.

I am, of course, deeply indebted to Professor Maslanka for introducing me, first, to teaching experiential courses and, second, to writing. No one could wish for a better guide and mentor, not only exceptionally skilled in both teaching and writing, but also long in patience and understanding.

I also offer my deep thanks to Professor Kelly, whose unique contributions brought a perspective I neither foresaw nor fully understood until she generously shared them.

—Nicole T. LeBoeuf

# BOARD OF ADVISORS

# TABLE OF CONTENTS

# Effective Communication for Lawyers

## Presenting, Counseling, Persuading

## CHAPTER 1

# PRESENTING

Lawyering is a social profession. Interactions with others is inevitable—whether speaking to a board of directors considering a merger, educating your child's class on career day, presenting a topic to a Continuing Legal Education (CLE) audience, or explaining a matter to a partner or associate.

While venues, purposes, and modalities differ, there is one constant: giving a cohesive presentation. Achieving cohesion rests, we suggest, in answering three questions facing all presenters:

*Question No. 1:* How do I immediately engage my audience?

*Question No. 2*: How do I sustain audience engagement?

*Question No. 3*: How do I convert that engagement into actionable take aways?

These answers provide an overarching structure in creating your presentation.

Now, step to the podium, the conference room table, the front of the room! You're on!

## I. COMMENCING

### The Challenge: How Do I Draft a Presentation?

Your inclination might be to proceed in a linear manner. After all, it is logical, and logic is invulnerable. For example, most will follow a formula as in: "I was asked to discuss Topic A. So, here are Facts L, M, and N. From these I arrived at Conclusion Z. Thank you for your attention."

But does this conventional method give the audience what it needs? Does it anchor their attention at the outset? Is it making the best use of your and the audience's time?

## Tool No. 1: Start at the End

Invert this conventional order and—to borrow a phrase—decide that "the last shall be the first." This tip comes from John Grisham, lawyer and novelist, who writes the ending of his novels first. So, in drafting a presentation consider starting at the end and working backwards.

### Tell and Show

In starting at the end, ask one overarching question: What message do you want the audience to walk away with?

Put more concretely: What do you want an audience member to say when their significant other at home or their colleague asks: "What was the talk about?"

Is it your goal for audience members to recite some facts they gleaned, or is it your goal for them to remember your *message*?

Note that "message" is singular. Just one, not multiple. A focused message is a memorable one. And that message must not be a gauzy aspiration—"I want to inspire my audience" or "I want to win support for my cause." Rather, it must be a concrete take away. Knowing your end point allows you to reverse-engineer the presentation, building towards it.

*Lesson: Know your destination before taking the first step.*

## Tool No. 2: Use a Throughline

A throughline tethers every part of the presentation to support your ultimate message. TED Talk creator Chris Anderson defines a throughline as "the connecting theme that ties together each narrative element" in a presentation. There are several methods to get you started on brainstorming what your throughline will be before you begin speaking.

## Tell and Show

### *Method No. 1: The Overarching Message*

Imagine: an organization such as The Rotary, the Chamber of Commerce, or your law school alumni association asks you to give a presentation on your recent summer vacation to Greece. You decide your message is: "Be courageous, make your travel dreams a reality." Consider the following options for how you can create a throughline with your message.

***Option A:***

Everyone should travel more. So, I fulfilled a lifelong dream and went to Greece. Let me tell you about the many beautiful buildings I saw there. Here is a slide of the Parthenon which commemorated the victory of Greece over Persia. It is an example of Doric Order Greek architecture . . .

*Option A* is a travel log, consisting solely of facts. They are unconnected silos. While perhaps interesting on their own, they do not deliver your message. This is a great way to lose your audience in facts without tying them together.

***Option B:***

As a child I read a book about the ancient Greeks. I loved the photos of the beautiful buildings and promised myself I would visit one day. I priced out a trip and saved every extra dollar to go. Ultimately, I was able to save enough to travel to Greece. It was even more beautiful than in my imagination. Let me tell you about planning to go, going, and lessons learned.

*Option B* takes those same facts and supports the throughline—through planning, patience, and imagination, anyone can achieve their childhood travel dreams. Every fact plays a role in delivering the overarching message of your presentation.

Here is a concrete illustration from a presentation by Professor Maslanka speaking at a Continuing Legal Education course on recent discrimination opinions from the United States Supreme Court. It could go one of two ways:

***Option A:***

In ABC case the Court relaxed the burden of proof by which a plaintiff must prove reverse discrimination. And in LMN case, the Court dropped a requirement that Title VII of the Civil Rights Act of 1964 requires an adverse employment action to be as severe as a termination or a denial of a promotion because of a protected classification. And, also, in XYZ case, the Court reversed a longstanding precedent that made it harder for an employer to establish an undue burden in providing a reasonable accommodation to an employee's religious beliefs.

*Option A* merely sets out the cases, leaving the listener to derive meaning. Again, it is made up of unconnected silos lacking an overarching structure. You don't need a lawyer to do this; the emerging technology of AI often does this when it strings facts together to give you an answer. It leaves the audience with the question, "Okay, and . . . ?"

***Option B:***

The last two terms of the Supreme Court demonstrate the power of the doctrine of textualism. When the Court determines the meaning of our anti-discrimination statutes, it uses the doctrine to come to its conclusion. In three cases—ABC, LMN, and XYZ—the Court used the doctrine to expand, not limit, employee rights.

In *Option B*, the same opinions are discussed but supported by a throughline—the doctrine of textualism is important to how the Court interprets employment laws—as a lawyer, you know this affects people's rights and obligations. The Court looks directly at the text to tease out the statute's meaning, and the speaker is in front of you to explain why that is important. Now, your audience can follow through the rest of your speech with your message in mind, knowing that each fact is there for a reason.

### *Method No. 2: The Three Question Method*

A throughline can be assembled by "The Three Question Method" developed by teacher Terry Borton. Ask yourself three questions while drafting your speech: "What?" "So What?" "Now What?":

**What?** Start with your message. You want to make sure that you articulate the "what" clearly and concisely, using key terms that you will reference throughout the presentation. This is the thread of your throughline. (More on the idea of the throughline in the next Challenge).

**So What?** Explain why your message matters in a connected narration. The audience is looking to you to say *why* your message matters. To deliver an effective message, your presentation cannot consist of unconnected silos. Connect the silos together, using facts in a narrative storyline to support your message and strengthen the spine of the throughline. This allows the audience to follow your message throughout the presentation.

**Now What?** This is where you personalize your message to the specific needs of *this* audience. What use can they make of the message? Is there something that you suggest they do to make the message meaningful in their lives? Can they share your message with others?

*Lesson: In whatever way you assemble your throughline, consider how each part of your talk reinforces or illuminates your ultimate message. Consider taking out facts or "silos" that are unconnected to your message.*

**The Neurodiversity Insight**

A throughline provides structure and, for neurodivergent individuals, structure is essential. For example, because of how quickly presenters with ADHD can make connections between concepts and ideas, they often need external organization to reiterate and draw them back to the "message." Oftentimes, when those with ADHD are asked a question that is tangential to the topic, they will answer it and continue delving into that concept and other related ideas, sometimes forgetting the original point. A throughline provides for them a useful reminder and guidance.

Neurodivergent individuals can also embrace tools other than a throughline in providing a structure to a presentation. Their challenge revolves around their belief that there is only "one" way to do something; that once a plan is set then it must move forward to completion; and that their focus is misunderstood as inflexibility.

- Do not become frustrated if the presentation is not unfolding as planned. Remember to slow down and not force the message.
- Do not become frustrated if you need to change the plan. Remind yourself that it is okay to take a detour and talk yourself through the new route to the end point.
- Do not believe that you have stalled out and will fall from the sky. Remind yourself of the power in taking a truly deep breath and re-regulating.

## Tool No. 3: Questions Are Your Friends

What is the most ideal time to consider an audience question?

(a) When it is asked

(b) At a post-presentation meeting

(c) Via personal email after the presentation

(d) Before the presentation is ever given

The correct answer is (d), before the presentation is ever given.

### Tell and Show

Questions are a speaker's friends. They allow—even require—interaction. To paraphrase a rule of politics, "a question is a terrible thing to waste." Let's start first with questions that you should ask yourself:

- **What does the audience already know?**

Think about your audience's background, interests, and level of knowledge on your topic. Always keep in the forefront of your mind this truth: while you may have lived with the facts or concepts in your head for a long time, these might be new or vaguely known by the audience. Effective lawyers are teachers, and effective teachers know that their own knowledge is a curse when it comes to explaining to others. It's important to spell it out to all audiences, so you meet them where they are. (We will re-visit this idea in the Persuasion section.)

- **What do you really know?**

Come to think of it, the foregoing question leads to this question. This might seem obvious. But effective communicators know that the more something supposedly goes without saying, the more it needs to be said. Knowledge changes very rapidly. Make sure yours is up to date.

- **What are the nuances of your message?**

Questions should be leveraged as an entry point in delivering your message, especially on any more subtle points you are trying to make. Do not merely say, "Thanks for the question" but "Thanks for that question and let me tell you and the audience why I am glad you asked it."

Now, let's shift gears and look at questions that will likely be asked by your audience. Anita Ramanathan, an award-winning speaker and former neuroscientist is a resource on this. She wrote a very helpful article "5 Steps to Anticipate Audience Questions and Prepare in Advance" (January 17, 2025) in her Word Cortex blog.

She writes in part that an audience will ask:

- **Questions to clarify**

During a presentation, audience members might want information on details.

*The Speaker Solution*: During your preparation think ahead to these 'how, what, and when' questions and be prepared to answer. Define terms of art, explain why you included the fact right after you include it, use dates and times, and keep it simple to resonate with the widest audience possible.

➢ **Questions that probe assumptions**

As you likely learned in evidence class, an objection is "assumes facts not on evidence." Here the audience picks up on a missing piece where you skipped over a predicate to your statement.

*The Speaker Solution*: Rehearse the presentation with a trusted colleague or friend, asking that they engage you in a Q and A session afterwards. It is even better to ask someone who is not in the legal field when asked to explain a complex area of law. This will help tease out any inadvertent assumptions about audience knowledge you may have made. Remember that it's best to repeat foreign concepts and engage with questioning faces to not lose members of your audience before you have reached the heart of your speech.

➢ **Questions that require reasons and/or evidence**

People may demand proof "Why do you say product A is better than product Z?" or 'Can you give me an example of where X caused Z?"

*The Speaker Solution*: Gather examples, case studies, or testimonials. Ask yourself: "What can I assemble that will be credible and will directly answer their question?" Take this book for example. We like to provide illustrations of the positive outcome that follows effective communication so it's digestible.

➢ **Questions about viewpoints and perspectives**

These questions are gold! Questions like these, in our opinion, demonstrate actual—as opposed to polite—interest. Audience members only ask them if they want to move forward or want to consider moving forward with your message. Illustrations would include "Is there an alternate to X?" or "What are the benefits of X?" or "With the constraints in time and budget, do you think X can work reliably?"

*The Speaker Solution*: In preparing to answer, Ramanathan suggests that you step into the future, asking yourself how your ideas can be of benefit to the questioner.

- **Questions that probe implications and consequences**

Again, pay dirt. These questions indicate active interest. They could be, "What happens if your cause does not get the funding you're looking for?" They are typically "what if" questions.

*The Speaker Solution*: Think about direct risks to the proposal in the presentation. While the answers you give will be speculative, focus on your preparation for giving a factual foundation for the speculation. This will bring you into predicting likelihood. It's like advocacy when you prepare to be rebutted by counsel opposite. You anticipate holes and use them to your advantage to show your superior knowledge and preparedness for going off script.

*Lesson: Plan well, speak well.*

## The Challenge: How Do I Start a Presentation?

How do I start a presentation, you ask? The answer is packaging. How you say something is just as important as what you say. The most successful retailers practice this truth.

Look at the Tiffany Blue Box for example. It is a light robin egg blue. The color was trademarked by Tiffany & Company in 1998 and has been synonymous with the brand since its first Blue Book catalog in 1845. The box is always adorned with a white satin ribbon, tied in a bow. The box packages, highlights, and enhances the item inside. It is instantly recognizable.

Take a page from Tiffany & Co.'s strategy with your presentation. Instead of "packaging," call it the "frame" of your presentation. Selection of the right frame is crucial because, as we see in the following chart, you only have a few minutes or so at the start of the presentation to initiate audience engagement. Each of the following three tools can help with "framing" your talk. Pick the one most suitable and most comfortable for you.

Consider the following chart. The horizontal axis represents the stage of a presentation while the vertical axis represents the audience's level of attention.

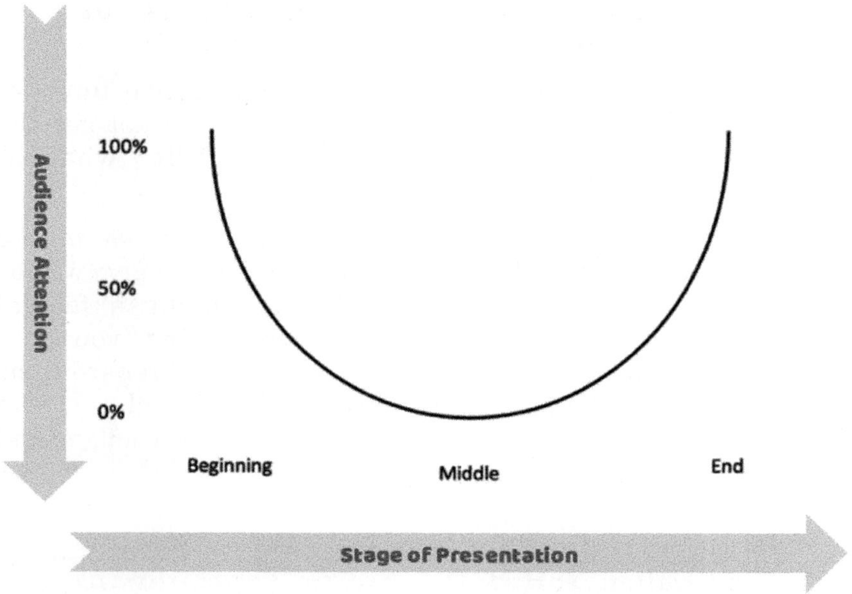


Our collective experience as speakers interprets the chart as meaning that you have—at most—*three minutes* at the start of the presentation to initiate audience engagement.

The question for you: How can I make a Tiffany-like first impression in my presentation, one that is engaging and memorable?

## Tool No. 1: B.L.U.F.

Here is the conventional wisdom: Presentations should be a pyramid, starting with a broad base of facts (The Five W's—Who, What, When, Where, and Why) leading up to the apex of the pyramid, the ultimate take aways. The conventional wisdom makes for an exhausting climb, and presents more like a mystery novel than a persuasive presentation.

### Tell and Show

Eliminate convention, adopt B.L.U.F. ("Bottom Line Up Front"). B.L.U.F. is standard operating procedure in the military (when in battle, it is best to get to the point first!). This communication method inverts this order and *starts* at the apex with your take-home point. While suspense is critical to a successful "whodunit", it impairs effective communication because the goal of a presenter is reducing the cognitive load of audience members. Put yourself in your audience's shoes and consider how much build-up is just the right amount before you lose focus.

Cognitive load theory, developed by pioneering educational psychologist John Sweller, says that learning is most efficient when our limited working memory is not overloaded. But the conventional pyramid increases this load and forces the listener to ask: "Where is the speaker going with this?" Their attention drops at the outset.

Starting with the "bottom line" circumvents this wasted effort by letting the audience know where you are going. You tell them the message when their attention (per the chart) is the most focused.

Here's a bonus tip: Consider starting with the needs of your audience using an audience-centric opener, "Today, you will learn about. . .", as opposed to a speaker-centric one, "Today, I will talk about. . .".

***By Way of Illustration:***

Let's look at this concept in practical terms. Compare *Option A* with *Option B*. Each illustrates a presentation to lawyers in a mid-sized city, asking them to contribute money to renovate the headquarters of the local bar association.

***Option A Start:***

"Thank you, Bar President Malik Lawyer and President-Elect Maria Esquire, for this opportunity to speak on an important topic. It is an honor to speak before such distinguished lawyers. We have long needed additional and more comfortable space for our events. Under the leadership of our current bar—and their predecessors—we are making progress toward such an expansion and renovation to meet the needs of our members."

***Option B Start:***

"Thanks to Bar leadership for this opportunity to speak about the expansion of our headquarters. We need to raise $50,000 to reach our goal of renovating and expanding our building. I will be suggesting three ways to get to $50,000 by the end of next year."

*Option B* works best. Remember: Audiences are very sensitive about their time being wasted, and they can be easily distracted by other thoughts (like wondering what's for dinner tonight) or stimuli (their smart phones). Use the B.L.U.F. to focus your audience on the message of your presentation.

*Lesson: Get to the point.*

## Tool No. 2: The "Cold Open"

A Cold Open is used in the performing arts. It is a narrative technique that simply dives into the material—no set-ups, no throat clearing, no thank you's.

Chances are you're already familiar with this concept, and it's often called the "hook" in literature. Shakespeare mastered the cold open in plays such as *Hamlet* and *MacBeth.* The perennial TV show Saturday Night Live starts every episode with a cold open. In whatever format, a Cold Open hooks its audience immediately by jumping directly into the action, with little or no context.

### Tell and Show

A Cold Open's purpose: "[I]t hooks your audience within the first few minutes . . . [A Cold Open] must be initially compelling, perhaps even surprising or unexpected, to grab your audience's attention from the get-go and convince them to stay." That's the incisive definition from L.A. blogger and writer Zan Romanoff, @zanopticon.

Let's say that you've been asked to give a talk to a group of professionals on the importance of having a final will and testament. *Option A* is a traditional starting frame. *Option B* is a non-traditional Cold Open consisting of a single question or a single declarative sentence.

***Option A:***

"Thank you for allowing me to speak today on the important topic of wills. We all know how important they are, but we all put off doing one. There are many factors to consider from legal and human perspectives."

***Option B:***

"Have you thought about dying?" or "We will all die."

Consider which Option grabs your attention the quickest and makes you want to know what comes next. Which Option would make your audience stop in their tracks?

*Lesson: In presenting, be entertaining.*

## Tool No. 3: The Cold Open as a Story

Another type of Cold Open is telling a very short story. The idea is launching the presentation with a specific story about a specific person, leveraging it into a broader, more universal context.

Back to Romanoff who advises that this technique "can be [a] delicate dance, you need to reveal enough information that the listener isn't confused. . .without giving away the whole story or bogging them down with exposition."

***By Way of Illustration:***

Let's say that a CLE talk is about the resources available for a new lawyer to draft a will. Here is one way you can do it:

1. *Set the Stage for the Conflict*

"Imagine this: Malik is sitting alone in his favorite Dallas coffee shop."

2. *Bridge to the Conflict*

"Malik has a job to do. He must write a will that a law firm partner instructed him to prepare. Sure, he took a Wills class in law school, but he has never written one!"

*3. Create the Conflict*

"Malik rubs his forehead, gets a double espresso, and asks himself 'How do I start? Where do I get the information?' "

*4. Resolve the Conflict*

"But Malik is not alone in this dilemma. Many of you may find yourself in the same circumstances. Here are resources and where you can find them."

You do not have to follow this scheme to a T. Every talk has its own dynamics, needs, and quirks. But using this template makes it easier to start and write a Cold Open that will leave the listeners in the audience wanting more.

*Lesson: Universalize your message through storytelling.*

### ***The Spotlight***

Does this Tool work? Check out this excerpt from Nobel Peace Prize recipient Malala Yousafzai's United Nations Speech on Youth Education, given in 2013 on her 16th birthday, where she uses the Cold Open to great effect:

> Dear Friends, on October 9, 2012, the Taliban shot me on the left side of my forehead. They shot my friends too. They thought that the bullets would silence us, but they failed. And out of that silence came thousands of voices. The terrorists thought that they would change my aims and stop my ambitions, but nothing changed in my life except this: Weakness, fear and hopelessness died. Strength, power and courage were born. I am the same Malala. My ambitions are the same. My hopes are the same. My dreams are the same.
>
> Dear sisters and brothers, I am not against anyone. Neither am I here to speak in terms of personal revenge against the Taliban or any other terrorist group. I am here to speak for the right for education of every child. I want education for the sons

> and daughters of the Taliban and all the terrorists and extremists.
>
> *[Editor's Note: Due to the formal setting, Malala spent valuable time at the start of her speech giving thanks to God and paying respect to the United Nations delegates. So, her cold open came later when she transitioned to the heart of the speech.]*

Here, Malala uses the Cold Open, not to state her message, but rather to grab the audience's attention. While the delegates likely paid professional courtesy to her opening formalities, we imagine that their attention really started to focus when she said, "I was shot. . . on the left side of my forehead."

## Tool No. 4: The Buffer

Perhaps Tools No. 1 and No. 2 are a bit too direct for you or for the audience. Again, all presentations are different. If too abrupt, consider using a buffer.

### Tell and Show

Think about your childhood swim lessons. It is unlikely that those lessons started with diving into the deep end of the pool. They likely started in the shallow end. You might not even have jumped in, but climbed in with a ladder or sat at the edge and eased your way in.

This analogy leads us to what we call "B.L.U.F. Plus." A B.L.U.F. or a Cold Open can be challenging for some audiences to process. Some audiences could become disoriented and confused. You do not want them to use their cognitive processing power asking themselves, "What is going on?"

Some audiences might even anticipate a message that they do not want to hear. A "Buffer" can help you explain or soften the message. (Not every talk is given to a friendly bar association consisting of sister and brother lawyers.) What follows is an historical example of "B.L.U.F. Plus".

### *The Spotlight*

It is July 14, 1948. The United States is a segregated country: our schools, our public transit, our lunch counters. You are in Philadelphia at the Democratic National Convention.

The delegates are having a fractious debate on whether they will advocate for a pro civil rights platform in the upcoming presidential election (for historical context, the Civil Rights Act was finally passed by Congress in 1964). Senator Hubert H. Humphrey spoke courageously in favor of its adoption, employing a "Buffer" to soften his message:

> *Mr. Chairman, fellow Democrats, fellow Americans:*
>
> *I realize that in speaking on behalf of the minority report on civil rights as presented by Congressman DeMiller of Wisconsin that I'm dealing with a charged issue—with an issue which has been confused by emotionalism on all sides of the fence. I realize that there are here today friends and colleagues of mine, many of them, who feel just as deeply and keenly as I do about this issue and who are yet in complete disagreement with me.*
>
> *My respect and admiration for these men and their views were great when I came to this convention. It is now far greater because of the sincerity, the courtesy, and the forthrightness with which many of them have argued in our prolonged discussions in the platform committee.*
>
> *Because of this very great respect—and because of my profound belief that we have a challenging task to do here—because good conscience, decent morality, demands it—I feel I must rise at this time to support a report—the minority report—a report that spells out our democracy, a report that the people of this country can and will understand, and a report that they will*

> *enthusiastically acclaim on the great issue of civil rights.*
>
> *Now let me say this at the outset that this proposal is made for no single region. Our proposal is made for no single class, for no single racial or religious group in mind. All the regions of this country, all the states have shared in our precious heritage of American freedom. All the states and all the regions have seen at least some of the infringements of that freedom—all people—get this—all people, white and black, all groups, all racial groups have been the victims at time[s] in this nation of—let me say—vicious discrimination.*

Do you see where he skillfully deployed his buffers?

He buffered because he knew that those who virulently disagreed with him would be listening intently at the outset, and second, because he did not want to alienate a delegate who might ultimately be persuaded. He is self-aware and it resonated with the audience.

Would he demonize them? No, he softens the blow by sincerely complimenting them. The compliment then acts as a transition, "Because of this very great respect. . ." and then he gives the B.L.U.F.: this is about "vicious discrimination."

*Lesson: Buffers must be sincere, heartfelt, believed. If they are not, they come off as inauthentic, patronizing and manipulative.*

## Tool No. 5: Establish Credibility

Credibility is created by seamlessly tying your life experiences to your topic. It cannot be established by proxy alone. Neither graduating from law school nor being a lawyer educates the audience on *why* they should sit through the presentation or *why* they should listen to you. How can you create credibility?

## Tell and Show

Before starting a presentation, you may be introduced by the event host who says something like:

> "Lola went to Boston University Law School after receiving her undergraduate degree in the classics from Brown University. She currently practices as a Senior Associate at ABC firm."

While these facts are important to you, they are not enough on their own to establish your credibility for the audience. Instead, think about building on them by blending your skill set or background into your introduction or your presentation.

***By Way of Illustration:***

> "I have served for seven years in the Solicitor General's office and handled six cases with issues involving the topic of my talk today."

As illustrated above, a great way to do this is through qualifying concepts that every person will understand, such as years of practice, intimacy with the topic at issue, and success.

Another indirect method of establishing your credentials is by mentioning your mentors or by using references to a shared experience. Civil rights champion Dr. Martin Luther King illustrated this when, in writing to a group of fellow ministers, he integrated quotes from the writings of the Apostle Paul, Saint Augustine, and Lutheran theologian and philosopher John Bunyan. The quotes came from a common educational canon familiar to the audience, showing that he was their peer and colleague, not just saying it.

Finally, credibility is about how you comport yourself. Come across as confident, not as a know-it-all. Remember that the people attending your presentation are open to being persuaded and do not want to be lectured. Being genuine, imperfect, and relatable is more persuasive than being too polished and rehearsed.

*Lesson: Let your life speak for you, not your stats.*

### Finding Your Voice

Now, let's practice drafting an opening of a presentation.

- Your daughter is in ninth grade. She asks you to come speak on Career Day. It's a short talk, no more than 10 minutes. Draft a one-paragraph opening. Consider your audience. Ask yourself: How can I use one of these tools to engage them?
- Your client is a defendant in a lawsuit. Liability is clear. A partner asks that you give a presentation to the client explaining their options, including settlement. Draw on your own experiences for the case facts. How should you start? Consider all options and then decide what tool is the most effective. Why?
- Your local bar association's CLE committee asks that you give an update on case law in your specialty. One group will be lawyers sharing your specialty, the other will be lawyers with a general practice. What is the difference between the openings to each group?
- Firms often have internal CLEs or firm meetings on cases that are being handled or have been resolved. Use B.L.U.F. to start your presentation. Try a "What?" "So, What?" "Now What?" structure. What questions might you expect to be asked? Plan for them.

## II. BRIDGING

### The Challenge: How Do I Sustain Audience Engagement?

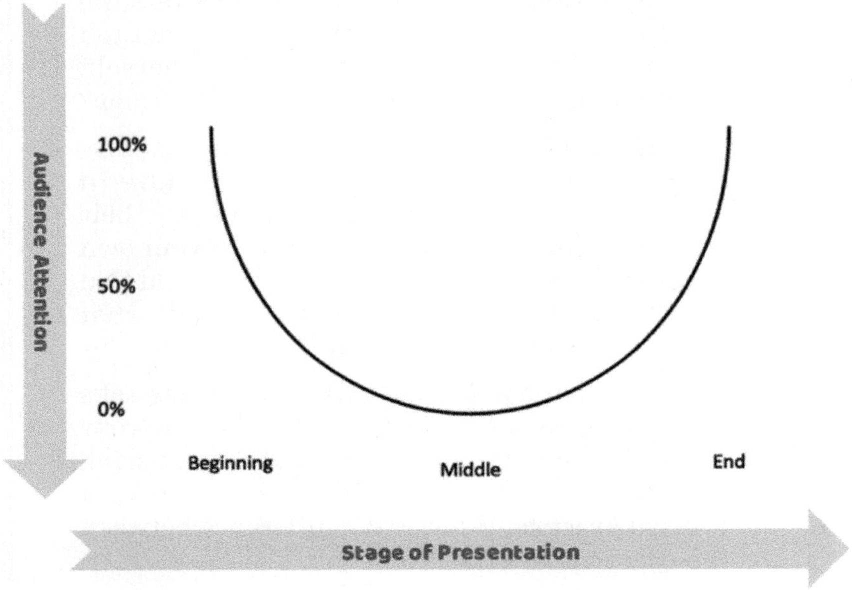


Recall our chart: Audience attention starts to lapse in the middle of your presentation. Once our minds become acclimated to a new situation, we relax because the familiar poses no threat. Active engagement decreases.

All well and good for the purpose of evolutionary biology but not so well and good for the purpose of continued audience engagement. This section suggests Tools to keep your audience engaged between commencement and closure.

### Tool No. 1: It's Always About the Audience

Lawyers and law students tend to shy away from absolutes. But here is one: "It's Always About the Audience" is for all presentations. It is never about the speaker. Period. While implementing this Tool, consider the following tips to ensure an audience-centric experience.

## Tell and Show

### ➢ Explain, Never Presume

We have visited this in previous Tools. Here, we will dive into more of the specifics. The biggest mistake speakers make is presuming that the audience knows more than they do. Steve Pinker, a cognitive researcher at Harvard University, calls this the "curse of knowledge." As he notes, "The better you know something, the less you remember about how hard it was to learn." You might have seen this in law school when a law professor started in the middle of a complex area of law, as opposed to laying the necessary groundwork for your comprehension.

### ➢ Be a Teacher, Not Merely an Expert

Professor Laura Webb picks up on the preceding point when she writes that "The effective professor educates her students by starting at their level of understanding and guiding them through doctrine and problem-solving steps, using not only her expertise in the topic but her understanding of pedagogy."

### ➢ Know the Lay of the Land

In preparing any presentation, you must understand that no two presentations are the same. Like every good general who prepares by learning the grounds on which the battle is to occur, you must scout out why the audience is there (the situational context), where the talk will be (the environmental context), and when you will be speaking (the psychological context).

**Situational Context:** You need to know why the audience is there because this is the *reason* why you are presenting. To do so, you might need some background on why they are interested in the subject or in you as the speaker. For example, imagine you've been invited to speak at the local Rotary Club about a new downtown redevelopment project. You do some quick research and find out that one of the Club's missions is to assist the downtown area's unhoused population. This should clue you in that they are expecting a talk about the new projects and how they will affect the unhoused persons living in downtown.

Their expectations must match the content of your talk or else audience engagement does not start effectively.

*Lesson: Know why your audience is there.*

**Environmental:** You also need to know where—the physical space in which you are presenting—the talk will be. A courtroom is different from a ballroom. In-person meetings are different from remote meetings (Zoom, Teams, etc.). Will you be standing up? At the front of a room? Outside? Will there be a place to lay down any notes? Will you be able to see the screen on which you will project your power point, image, or document? Environment really matters. For example, Professor Maslanka gave a talk in a large ballroom which was filled only a third of the way with audience members and two thirds of the room was empty. He felt off balance and the talk suffered.

*Lesson: Consider how your audience views you from a third-party perspective.*

**Psychological:** Finally, you need to know when your speech is taking place, so that you can consider the current state of your audience's values and needs. These psychological factors will impact whether they fully comprehend and absorb what you are saying. Think about timing. Are you speaking at the end of a long conference or right before lunch? Are you kicking off the conference with your presentation, or closing it down on a drowsy Friday afternoon? Remember: It's Always About the Audience! Plan your speech to meet their needs accordingly. This principle translates to the following tips. Hungry audience members may need more signposts in your presentation ("and now, for my third and final point. . .") while Friday attendees want to know your plan to be finished before rush hour begins and will need to know that you have an important and valuable message that makes this final stretch of attendance worthy of their attention. Create a roadmap for them.

*Lesson: Never forget it's about the audience, not you.*

- **Include, Never Exclude**

Your audience is much more likely to stay engaged if they connect with you as a speaker. Steven D. Cohen, of the Harvard Division of Continuing Education, advises that: "One of the easiest ways to bond with your audience is to use inclusive pronouns like *we, our,* and *us,* instead of *you* and *your.*" Consider using these pronouns and other inclusive language to foster trust and connection with the audience.

***The Spotlight***

Giving a presentation to C-level executives—such as the CEO, the CFO, the CLO (a/k/a General Counsel), and the CMO (Chief Marketing Officer) can be both an exhilarating and intimidating experience. This is especially true if you are pitching you and your team's ideas to them. An article in the Harvard Business Review, "How to Blow a Presentation to the C-Suite," October 17, 2018, by business coach Sabina Nawaz got us thinking about the topic as it serves as an illustration of always keeping your audience in mind.

Here are some actionable pointers from the article and our experiences.

- **Pointer No. 1: It Is About a Problem, Not Your Idea**

It is the problem, not your solution that executives want to hear first. Context is everything. Your idea gets more attention if the executives can see that it solves a pressing problem or will become more significant without their attention.

- **Pointer No. 2: Speak to Executives in a Language They Understand**

Executives will ask challenging questions, but see that as a positive. In her article, Nawaz writes: "Rapid-fire, blunt questions are a sign that executives are interested in your idea. They're processing what you said, testing various angles and hypotheses, and generally want to learn more." (Similar to judges in the courtroom.) Silence is not a sign they are stunned by your brilliance. They seek direct answers to their direct questions, not a "on the one hand this and on the other hand that." We will delve more into how to communicate to this style when we discuss the Birkman test in Section II.

➢ **Point No. 3: Offer a Return on Investment**

Always speak to people in a language they can understand. Here, high level executives will always want to know answers to the following questions:

- ➢ Will the idea pay for itself in a certain period of time?
- ➢ Will the idea generate revenues or reduce expenses? If so, what are the numbers?
- ➢ Any expenses for the idea and its set-up?

*Lesson: It is only human nature to be excited by your idea. But don't fall in love with it. By doing so, you lose the objectivity needed to effectively communicate, especially with C-level executives.*

## Tool No. 2: The Power of Contrast

Have you ever scrolled through social media and come across a TikTok with a familiar "before and after" theme? The first clip of the video is a "Before Shot" showing something undesirable; then comes the "After Shot," and a dramatic transformation. The transformative agent is whatever is being sold by the video's author. Simple formula? Yes. Effective? You bet.

### Tell and Show

How do our minds work? All of us are quick to make assumptions and jump to conclusions, often unconsciously and often based on too little information. Our brains are wired to do this because we do not have the time or energy to understand everything we see and encounter. We make an implicit assumption without recognizing that there is a gap or hole in our understanding.

Psychologist Daniel Kahneman explained in his book *Thinking, Fast and Slow* that we need the fast-thinking part of our brain so we can automatically react when faced with danger. The human race is 300,000 years old. Early humans faced dangers almost constantly, so the principal purpose of our brains was to help us survive by being finely attuned to our environment.

Imagine this: Our distant ancestors are walking across the plains of the Serengeti. You are the person taking the point for the group, you see green grass, green grass, green grass, brown lion. . . Run! Even if the "lion" turns out to be brown grass, your reaction is immediate. Fast-forward thousands of years: while the need has diminished, the wiring is the same.

What does this have to do with presenting? In 1986, a groundbreaking work was published in the American Journal of Sociology by John Heritage and David Greatbatch. They took 476 political speeches, seeking a prediction metric of what was said in the speech that triggered audience applause. Nineteen thousand sentences later, they reached this conclusion: A significant number of audiences applauded when contrast was used by the speaker.

As Nancy Duarte points out in her book, *Resonate: Present Visual Stories That Transform Audiences*, contrast creates contour (or as we like to say, "provides texture") that an audience can cling to. The more the audience clings, the greater the chance your message will stick. Duarte writes:

"People are naturally attracted to opposites, so presentations should draw from this attraction to create interest. Communicating an idea juxtaposed with its opposite creates energy. Moving back and forth between the contradictory poles encourages full engagement from the audience." Duarte believes speakers should pull an audience from "what is" to "what could be."

Duarte suggests using the following contrasts in making your points. By way of example, use opposing words to structure your presentation. These contrasts bring your idea full circle.

| Past/present | Future |
|---|---|
| Need | Fulfillment |
| Speed | Endurance |
| Ambition | Humility |
| Stagnation | Growth |
| Budget | Quality |

*Lesson: We are biologically wired for contrast. Use it.*

### *The Spotlight*

It is 1962, and you are attending President Kennedy's speech at Rice University in Houston, Texas. He announces a goal of the United States-to put a man on the moon by the end of the decade. Here is President Kennedy:

> *We meet in an hour of change and challenge, in a decade of hope and fear, in an age of both knowledge and ignorance. The greater our knowledge increases, the greater our ignorance unfolds. No man can fully grasp how far and how fast we have come [. . .]*
>
> *We choose to go to the moon. We choose to go to the moon in this decade and do the other things, not because they are easy, but because they are hard.*

Note the dynamic contrasts that he uses—change and challenge, hope and fear, knowledge and ignorance—and how they propel the talk forward. He also uses an antithesis, a form of contrast consisting of "Not X, but Y" as in "Not because it is easy, but because they are hard." Simple enough to say, "because it is hard" and leave it at that but contrasting it in this manner with "easy" serves to underscore the message. This tool is easy to implement because you can use contrast by simply putting two contrasting words near each other in a sentence.

***By Way of Illustration:***

Here is a concrete illustration of this method in action. A young person goes to a hair salon because their hair has been ruined by at-home bleach. The hairdresser takes a video to show how the client's hair improved after treatment.

In the first clip, the client's hair looks ruined, damaged, frizzy, and miscolored.

In the second clip, the client's hair looks smooth, frizz-free, and the color is seamlessly blended as if she never damaged her hair at all.

The Transformative Agent: the hairdresser's magical touch and skill.

*Lesson: This tool is as easy as 1, 2, 3. Give it a spin.*

## Tool No. 3: Be Concrete

There are multiple benefits to the use of concrete words and phrases: imprinting memorable images, increasing retention of facts, strengthening identification with your throughline.

### Tell and Show

We can learn a lot from other professions. Here is a teaching moment from the world of business. In a recent experiment on customer satisfaction, Wharton School of Business Professor Jonah Berger found that using concrete language increased customer satisfaction because, regardless of the outcome, use of concrete language made it easier for people to understand how their questions were being addressed and resolved.

Imagine a scenario where a shoe salesperson is waiting on a customer who asks to buy a pair of sneakers with a very specific color combination. Which employee response is the most effective?

(a) "I will look for them."

(b) "I will look for those shoes."

(c) "I will find those lime green Nikes with orange soles."

Or imagine this scenario provided by Professor Maslanka, who ordered customized tee shirts for one of his classes via a 1-800 number. He called to follow up on the delivery location. What is their most effective response to him?

(a) "The package will be arriving at your location."

(b) "The package will be arriving at your home."

(c) "The package will be arriving at your door."

The answer to both scenarios is C. The continuum of answers increasingly becomes more concrete and thus more memorable. The customer is left with a positive impression, not an amorphous aspiration. As with customers, so too with audience members/listeners.

Here is a bonus benefit: being concrete facilitates our ability to process and recall information so it ensures your audience isn't making inferences different from what you intend. Simply put, we are better able to process concrete words. Here is a chart demonstrating this principle:

| Abstract | Concrete |
|---|---|
| Transportation | Car |
| Illumination | Lamp |
| Food | Hamburger |

*Lesson: When in doubt, pick the concrete.*

### *The Spotlight*

Let's see how this principle plays out in effective communication. Remember, it is 1962, you are attending President Kennedy's speech at Rice University in Houston, Texas. Kennedy was urged by NASA to use this throughline: "Our goal is to be preeminent in space." Rejecting this as meaningless, he opted for this: "Our goal is to put a man on the moon and return him safely." With this overview, he then said:

*[. . .] But condense, if you will, the 50,000 years of man's recorded history in a time span of but a half a century. Stated in these terms, we know very little about the first 40 years, except at the end of them, advanced man had learned to use the skins of animals to cover them.*

*Then about 10 years ago, under this standard, man emerged from his caves to construct other kinds of shelter. Only five years ago, man learned to write and use a car with wheels. Christianity began less than two years ago. The printing press came this year. And then less than two months ago, during this whole 50-year span of human history, the steam engine provided a new source of power. Newton explored the meaning of gravity. Last month, electric lights and telephones and automobiles and airplanes became available. Only last week did we develop penicillin and television and nuclear power [. . .] This is a breathtaking pace, and such a pace cannot help but create new ails as it dispels old [. . .]*

*So, it is not surprising that some would have us stay where we are a little longer, to rest, to wait [. . .] If this capsuled history of our progress teaches us anything, it is that man in his quest for knowledge and progress is determined and cannot be deterred.*

*[. . .] We shall send to the moon 240,000 miles away [. . .], a giant rocket, more than 300 feet tall [. . .] on an untried mission to an unknown celestial body and then return it safely to Earth. But why some say the moon? Why choose this as our goal? And they may well ask, why climb the highest mountain? Why 35 years ago fly the Atlantic? Why does Rice play Texas?*

*We choose to go to the moon. We choose to go to the moon in this decade and do the other things not because they are easy, but because they are hard. Because that goal will serve to organize and measure the best of our energies and skills, because that challenge is one that we're willing to accept. One we are unwilling to postpone. And therefore, as we set sail, we ask God's blessing on the most hazardous and dangerous and greatest adventure on which man has ever embarked.*

Broken down, here is an illustration of the differences:

**The Abstract:** "We will launch a man in a rocket to the moon and return him home safely."

**The Concrete:** "We shall send a rocket to the moon 240,000 miles away [. . .], a giant rocket, more than 300 feet tall [. . .] on an untried mission to an unknown celestial body and then return it safely to Earth [. . .]"

The concrete language in this example is visual, the speaker emphasizes how large this mission is through numbers. It leaves a lasting impression in the audience's minds.

**The Abstract:** "We make ourselves better by accepting and overcoming challenges."

**The Concrete:** "[W]hy climb the highest mountain? Why 35 years ago fly the Atlantic? Why does Rice play Texas (in foot ball)?"

The concrete language is an example of other feats and challenges that mankind has faced that are familiar with the audience. The last one, while not the same as climbing a mountain or sending a rocket into space, is personal for residents of Texas and shows that even the smallest wins, like a football game, are indicative of why humans face challenges at all.

**The Abstract:** "It is good that we set goals for ourselves."

**The Concrete:** "We choose to go to the moon in this decade and do the other things not because they are easy but because they are hard. (Note the power of contrast here with easy/hard.) Because that goal will serve to measure the best of our energies and skills . . ."

This concrete language should resonate with people who have challenged themselves to be the best and illustrate more than just "set goals", an overused concept, as in the Abstract.

*Lesson: The concrete makes for vivid, memorable, and actionable messages. In a world of abstractions, be concrete.*

## Tool No. 4: Use Data

Always consider integrating data into your presentation. Doing so demonstrates you've done your homework; supports your message with evidence (enhancing credibility); adds a dose of realism; and embeds in audience members an easy to recall talking point. Think back to the Spotlight above when President Kennedy used the size of the rocket and the distance in miles to space to make his speech more concrete.

### Tell and Show

Conventional wisdom says cold numbers shouldn't evoke emotions, but conventional wisdom is wrong. Consider the following Abstract v. Concrete example from Professor Lynn Meade at the University of Arkansas who teaches us how to effectively use the concrete principle when talking about numbers.

- **Tip No 1: Pick the Concrete over the Abstract**

Which Option packs a punch?

***Option A*:**

"According to the United Nations, many children in sub-Saharan Africa do not receive a basic education to learn reading and writing skills."

***Option B*:**

"In sub-Saharan Africa, one in five children between six and eleven are not in school. In addition, of those youths aged 15–16, 60% are not in school. What does this mean? To put in perspective, consider if over half of your high school class was denied access to school."

It is *Option B*. There, use of data brings a reality to the point sought to be made. And the reference to high school makes the point relatable to the audience member and further underscores the message. We will re-visit this concept in Persuasion.

### ➢ Tip No. 2: Use Ballpark Data (Mostly)

To lessen the cognitive strain on the audience, be sure to ballpark a number as opposed to using a specific number. With President Kennedy's speech, he rounded up 238,855 miles to 240,000 miles. Using 238,855 would result in a cognitive hiccup; the more accurate number causing the listener to waste a precious few seconds to process what the number means, interrupting the flow of the speech. It simply takes longer to process a detailed number than to process a more general number. (One exception: use a very specific number if the purpose of using data is developing credibility.) Purpose drives use.

### ➢ Tip No. 3: Billboard What Is Coming

Numbers change the pacing of a speech. The audience hears "words, words, words" and then up pops a number. Too abrupt. To battle this, "billboard" a number that is coming, not unlike seeing a highway sign that says, "Next Rest Stop in 5 Miles." Try the following:

- "I am now going to give you a number that will surprise you."
- "Let me shift gears now and use some data to highlight my point."
- "And the data support this view. . ."

Think of these "micro transitions" as buffers of sorts, easing the cognitive load for the listener.

### ➢ Tip No. 4: Slow Down, Then Vary for Emphasis

We normally process a number by seeing it on the printed page. Because verbalizing numbers is the exception, not the rule, our brains need more time to process a heard number. A very effective technique is using the *same* number but in *different* contexts. Professor Meade gives a great example of skillful repetition, as opposed to pointless redundancy, that we've slightly altered:

> According to a study conducted by the National Center for Education Statistics, 1 in 5 adults has low literacy skills. One in five (*pause*). . . let that sink in for a

moment. Let's put that into perspective: 1 in 5 adults struggles to read a newspaper, a job application, a medical form. 1 in 5 lacks the ability to read things that would allow them to engage in society.

Note: she repeats the numbers several times to emphasize how shocking that should be for the audience. 1 in 5 sounds insignificant without the added explanation of how large that is for the concept of literacy. She emphasizes the importance of this number through her illustration of how literacy impacts an adult's everyday life, and in turn, their entire life. Therefore, 1 in 5 adults turns into a central point of the speech, and the audience will take away this knowledge after the speech is over because it is a simple and concrete statistic to remember. Without the repetition, 1 in 5 is a forgotten point.

➢ **Tip No. 5: Translate Numbers into Relatable Terms**

Let's stay with relatability for a minute. Data does not speak for itself. It is up to the speaker to translate numbers into comprehensible concepts for the listener.

The goal is limiting cognitive drain on the listener. Our brains have a cognitive limit so that at some point a number is so large it loses all meaning, becoming so much white noise. 100 miles? Got it. 5 miles? Clear. 43 million miles? Glazed eyes. Check out supporting scholarship in "To Put That in Perspective: Generating Analogies That Make Numbers Easier to Understand" by Riederer, Hofman, Goldstein.

Groundbreaking work in this tip is discussed by Chip Heath and Karla Starr in "*Making Numbers Count: The Art and Science of Communicating Numbers.*" One of their insights: know the number but do not use it. Rather, translate it so that the number is represented by an image or concept.

Let's say your talk is about how little drinkable water the world contains. It is a life-or-death situation. The authors above advise to avoid using large numbers because they are too much for the human brain to comprehend, no matter how powerful or how accurate. The audience member would have to imagine all of the water in the world—oceans, seas, lakes, streams, etc.—and then split it into percentages in their head. That's not useful for your illustration in this particular speech, as it was in the literacy example. Instead, translate it into a vivid, concrete, meaningful example of how large that really is. Consider the following:

**Accurate, Not Memorable**

***Option A:***

97.5% of the world's water is salinized and thus undrinkable. Of the 2.5% that is fresh, over 99% is trapped in glaciers and snow fields. Thus, in total, only 0.25% of the water on the globe is drinkable by humans and animals.

**Accurate and Memorable**

***Option B:***

Imagine a gallon jug filled with water and three ice cubes. All of the water in the jug is salt water. The ice cubes are the only fresh water, and humans can only drink the drops that are melting off each.

Heath and Starr, the authors above, advise to think like you are an audience member and consider, "If you're not a numbers person, the gallon jug translation is instantly more approachable. In the first translation, when you see all the percent signs and the small decimal, you may go into panic mode."

This is yet another example of ballparking that we spoke about with reference to the distance of the moon from earth.

*Lesson: Assess what your concept is, whether numbers fit into it or if it will fly over your audience's head, and adapt. Either way, be visual and concrete.*

## Tool No. 5: Engage the Audience

Ideally a presenter should aspire to some form of two-way communion with the audience. However you do so, think in advance of the communication techniques you can use in engaging the audience. This Tool discusses ways of continuing the engagement.

## Tell and Show

➢ **Tip No. 1: Engage at the Outset.**

Communications consultant Doug Neff often asks a question in his first 60 seconds of a presentation. He likes to ask the audience a simple question about themselves, then asks them to respond by raising their hands ("Raise your hands if you've ever been . . .").

➢ **Tip No. 2: Make the Audience Members the Star**

Here is another angle from communication coach Craig Valentine who says that "[W]hen you find ways to make individuals in your audience the stars of your speech; you automatically connect deeply with the group." Sometimes this is because others in the group will engage vicariously, considering their own response to the question posed, other times it's because it adds variation to the talk.

➢ **Tip No. 3: Use Names**

Finally, cognitive theory teaches us that our brains respond to our names. Hearing one's name activates the *medial prefrontal* region of the brain, which processes thoughts about oneself and is involved in self-referential tasks. A direct linkage to our sense of self.

Here are some additional payoffs:

➢ *Recognition and Validation*

Hearing one's name signals that the person matters, and that attention is being paid to them (and by extension, the audience).

➢ *Neurotransmitters Are Released*

Dopamine and serotonin are hormones that trigger feelings of well-being and pleasure. Thus, an audience that is more receptive to your throughline message.

➢ **Tip No. 4: Use Inclusive Framing**

People must feel competent to comment. So, do not ask, "Can you tell us about the best meal you ever had?" instead of "Can you tell us about a good meal?" The formula: the less cognitive processing power that must be expended by the audience member, the more engaged the audience member.

- **Tip No. 5: Strategically Use Slides**

We tend to discourage the use of Power Point slides because the audience focuses on the slide and not on what you are saying. And a slide too full of information results in you speaking on one part of the slide as the audience reads ahead on another part of the slide. If you do use slides, Neff encourages audience engagement by stopping at an effective or useful slide, pausing and stating "Okay, everyone, take out your smartphones. This is the slide you want to take home with you." Yet another example of a call-and-response with your audience.

- **Tip No. 6: Use a Prop**

The use of physical, tangible props or visual aids engages the audience. Pull it out and their attention perks up; their minds go to, "Gee what is this?" Anticipation leads to effective communion. Check out Jill Bolte Taylor's TED Talk "*My Stroke of Insight*" in which she uses a human brain model to show what happens during a stroke. Imagine the talk *without* its use.

Or take Professor Maslanka's video, "Have a Beer with A Stranger" here, in which he talks about a random encounter in a bar with a person studying mixed martial arts. She told him of three lessons taught by her instructor which Professor Maslanka then applies to legal practice. The prop? He starts off by showing a pair of mixed martial arts gloves, asking what they are, and then saying, "And why am I showing them to you?" The hope is that the audience thinks "Tell us more." Here is a link to Professor Maslanka's video: https://bit.ly/useaprop.

Embrace the unusual, different, offbeat.

- **Tip No. 7: Acknowledge Contributions**

We all like to be sincerely praised. Do so here even if it is only a "thank you." As you develop your skills as a speaker, you can—like a good law school professor—frame your response to your throughline and refer back to the audience's contributions in your close.

*Lesson: Want to learn more about these tools? We recommend checking out "5 Tips for Powerful Audience Participation" by Jesse Scinto, in his "Fast Company" article. (April 15, 2014)*

## Tool No. 6: Do Questions Work?

A powerful tool in presentations is phrasing a statement as a question, commonly known as a "rhetorical question." As with other powerful tools—use sparingly, deploy intentionally, insert strategically.

### Tell and Show

Chances are that you are already familiar with the power of rhetorical questions. At some point in your education, you may have read "The Merchant of Venice," Shakespeare's timeless play on mercy, justice, and prejudice. (Some literary scholars consider the play as anti-Semitic; others consider it an early plea for tolerance. We condemn anti-Semitism whenever or wherever it occurs, using the play solely for its use of rhetorical questions.) Shylock, hated and vilified for being a wealthy Jew, argues to a judge that a non-Jewish Venetian citizen breached an ironclad contract with him. Believing the deck is stacked against him in court, he argues:

> "If you prick us, do we not bleed? If you tickle us, do we not laugh? If you poison us, do we not die? And if you wrong us, shall we not seek revenge?"

This technique was popularized over 2,000 years before Shakespeare in Aristotle's "Art of Rhetoric." A rhetorical question's purpose? To prompt reflection by the listener. Consider Shakespeare's questions. Let's compare them as Statements v. Questions:

Statements:

- By pricking us, we will bleed.
- Tickling us makes us laugh.
- Give us poison, and we will die.
- Do a wrong against us, and we will seek retribution.

Questions:

- If you prick us, do we not bleed?
- If you tickle us, do we not laugh?
- If you poison us, do we not die?
- If you wrong us, do we not seek revenge?

The intent is the same, but which is more effective? When phrased as rhetorical questions, the listeners become engaged, ideas are emphasized, reflection triggered.

What cognitive functions are enlisted by a rhetorical question? When we hear a rhetorical question, our brains start searching for answers even though we know no answer is expected. The question imprints itself on our minds, making it memorable and, forcing us to answer, making us engage.

A 2004 study conducted by Cognitive Researchers Daniel J. Howard and Rogers A. Kerin revealed that "elaborative processing," results from their use, meaning that a listener is not only more likely to consider the issue presented, but to more deeply consider it. Other researchers found that rhetorical questions engage listeners with little prior interest in the topic.

Moreover, speaking coach Dzigbordi Kwaku-Dosoo writes in her column, "The Power of Rhetorical Questions in Public Speaking: A Deep Dive into A Masterful Technique" that these questions reinforce "key points" and encourage "the audience to retain information long after the speech ends." Why? Because the speaker draws specific attention to the answer.

This is especially useful when tapping into the audience's emotions. We will return to the use of questions in the Persuasion section of this book, but here is a short example for now. Imagine you are arguing that your client's due process rights were violated. Consider saying: "What would become of us as a country if due process disappeared?" or "What would become of us as a country if a court order was ignored by the government?" or "What would become of our country if a legal decision determined by the richest litigant?"

*Lesson: Immediate hook, immediate engagement.*

### *The Spotlight*

You are still at President Kennedy's speech at Rice University in Houston, Texas. You are a student at Rice, who has never missed a home football game. As a Rice football fan, your archenemy (and the college football powerhouse) is the University of Texas, often referred to as "Texas." Here is President Kennedy:

> *We shall send to the moon 240,000 miles away, a giant rocket, more than 300 feet tall [. . .] on an untried mission to an unknown celestial body and then return it safely to Earth. But why some say the moon? Why choose this as our goal? And they may well ask, why climb the highest mountain? Why 35 years ago fly the Atlantic? Why does Rice play Texas?*

The last question was unnecessary but very effective for that audience. Everyone in that audience now understood exactly the point President Kennedy was making. He drew a personal analogy to which this specific audience could relate. By the end of the speech, he personalized a national message and built a connection with every Rice football fan in the audience. The Rice/Texas reference works because everyone in the audience knew of the rivalry and of the lopsided advantages of football powerhouse Texas over Rice.

We again see the powerful use of rhetorical questions coupled with a common language in "Letter from a Birmingham Jail" by civil rights leader Dr. Martin Luther King. Dr. King was imprisoned for civil disobedience in protesting segregated conditions in the South. He wrote from jail a response to statements by other ministers that his actions were "unwise and untimely." Note how he masterfully sets up his argument by using a rhetorical question.

> *One of the basic points in your statement is that the action that I and my associates have taken in Birmingham is untimely. Some have asked "Why*

> *didn't you give the new city administration time to act?" [. . .] For years now, I have heard the word "Wait!" It rings in the ear of every Negro with piercing familiarity. This "Wait" has almost always meant "Never." We must come to see . . . "that justice too long delayed is justice denied." We have waited more than 340 years for our constitutional God given rights.*

Dr. King's rhetorical question, presented as a question "some have asked," leaves cognitive space for the reader to consider the question themselves, as they are not being directly challenged to answer it. In giving their answer some thought, perhaps even forming their own reply, the reader is primed to hear the ultimate and resounding response that the wait has already lasted for more than three centuries, while further waiting is itself an injustice.

> *One may well ask 'How can you advocate breaking some laws and obeying others?' The answer lies in the fact that there are only two types of law: just and unjust. I would be the first to advocate obeying just laws. Conversely, one has a moral responsibility to disobey unjust laws. [. . .]*
>
> *In your statement you assert that our actions, even though peaceful, must be condemned because they precipitate violence. But is this a logical assertion? Isn't this like condemning a robbed man because his possession of money precipitated the evil act of robbery? [. . .]*
>
> *And now this approach is being termed extremist [. . .] Was not Jesus an extremist for love? [. . .] Was not Amos an extremist for justice? Was not Paul an extremist for the Christian gospel?*

If Dr. King had only used simple declarative statements, the power of engagement would never have been triggered. By asking these questions, the reader (or a listener) internally embraces the message being delivered.

*Lesson: When people convince themselves, they stay convinced.*

Finally, note how Dr. King sets up his argument but first frames the question in the terms of an argument from the other side.

That's the difference between a person directing you to a belief by pointing their finger and a person persuading you to a belief by leading you to generate your own answers. That's when people are truly convinced.

Elaborative processing: make it work for you.

## Tool No. 7: Generate Questions from the Audience

Scholar Daniel Pink (@DanielPink on X, formerly Twitter) introduced the authors to former law professor Ozan Varol, author of the book, *Awaken Your Genius*, and to this gem of how to generate questions ensuring audience engagement.

*Don't Ask*: "Does anyone have any questions?"

This seems like a smart move. The speaker is inviting questions, opening themselves and their message to scrutiny. A question and answer are the best way to engage are they not? Yes, but only if the request actually prompts questions. Professor Varol discovered that asking *this* question produces silence, crickets, zero engagement.

*Do Ask*: "What I just lectured on might seem confusing. I'm sure a bunch of you have questions. Now's the time to ask."

The result was totally different. Hands shot up. Why? Pink explains that the latter communicated three things:

- Normalizes any confusion
- Creates psychological safety
- Makes it okay to "not get it."

In short, human nature is that none of us want to look dumb or weak. This simple reframe eliminates this hostage to fear. Here is Pink: "Change your framing. Change the room. Change the outcomes."

We will revisit this issue when we talk about counseling clients in Section II.

*Lesson: Small things matter. Like football, effective communication is often a game of inches.*

## Tool No. 8: The Rule of Three

All presentations need a unifying technique to pull together their disparate elements into a single, unifying theme. Enter the rule of three.

### Tell and Show

You will quickly recognize this rule:

- "Life, Liberty, and the Pursuit of Happiness" from Jefferson's Declaration of Independence
- Newton's Three Laws of Motion
- "Snap, Crackle, Pop"
- Swearing in a witness: "The truth, the whole truth—and nothing but the truth"
- "Oyez! Oyez! Oyez!" proclaimed by the marshal at the start of each United States Supreme Court session.

None of this is coincidental. It's planned.

This Tool, like others in this book, is based on cognitive science. In 1956, a groundbreaking study was conducted at Bell Labs by Harvard researcher George Miller. He discovered that contrary to conventional wisdom, our short-term memory can only hold a limited amount of information. Further research determined the optimal number is three! More on the concept later in the book.

Roy Peter Clark, a scholar at The Poynter Institute for Media Studies, in his article, "Writing Tools: 55 Essential Strategies for Every Writer," expands on this insight. Try saying them out loud:

- The Father, the Son, and the Holy Spirit
- Moe, Larry, and Curly
- A priest, a minister, and a rabbi
- The executive, legislative, and judicial branches
- The Niña, the Pinta, and the Santa Maria
- The way, the truth, the life
- Breakfast, lunch, dinner
- Beginning, middle, end

Clark observes that the magic number "three" provides a greater sense of completeness than "two" or "four." "Three" is a holistic number. His point? Three words give us completeness, wholeness, and roundness. (One and two words have their place. For example: use one word to make a powerful statement and two words for comparison and contrast.)

Professor Patrick Barry's article "The Rule of Three" appears in *Legal Communication & Rhetoric:* JALWD, Vol. 15 (2018): 247–61. Professor Barry insightfully writes that there are two types of the Rule of Three: "Same, Same, Kind of Different" and "Short, Short Kind of Long."

**Type No. 1: Same, Same, Kind of Different**

He writes that the slogan of the sandwich franchise Jimmy John's uses this structure, "Fresh, Fast, Tasty" as does the slogan of Big Law firm Sidley Austin LLP, "Talent. Teamwork. Results." The first two words are similar and reinforce one another, while the third word is the punch line resulting from the first two.

**Type No. 2: Short, Short, Kind of Long**

Think of "Life, Liberty, and the Pursuit of Happiness" or the U.S. Marines Corp slogan "The few. The proud. The Marines." (two syllables, two syllables, three syllables). In this type, the third clause in its entirety is the conceptual punch line.

We would add the following:

**Type No. 3: Same, Same, Same, Punchline**

We saw this Type in the quoted passage from The Merchant of Venice. The first three questions are of a type, two serious (bleeding and death), the third not so serious (tickled laughter), with all three using the same underlying structure. The three funnel into the take home point ("If you wrong us. . .").

***The Spotlight***

Imagine you are at the Oscars. The actor Matthew McConaughey just received an Academy Award of Merit (the "Oscar") for Best Actor. You are a developing communications expert and, naturally, will be attuned to the structure of his acceptance speech. Spot how many times he uses the Rule of Three:

> *Thank you, to the other nominees. All these performances were impeccable in my opinion. I didn't see a false note anywhere.*
>
> *[. . .]*
>
> *There are a few things—about three things, to my count, that I need each day. One of them is something to look up to; another is something to look forward to; and another is someone to chase.*
>
> *Now, first off, I want to thank God because that's who I look up to. [. . .] In the words of the late Charlie Laughton who said, "When you got God, you got a friend, and that friend is you."*
>
> *To my family—that's who and what I look forward to:*
>
> *To my father, who I know he's up there right now with a big pot of gumbo; he's got a lemon meringue pie over there; he's probably in his underwear, and he's got a cold can of Miller Lite and he's dancing right now. To you dad—you taught what it means to be a man.*

> *To my mother, who's here tonight, who taught me and my two older brothers—demanded—that we respect ourselves. And what we in turn learned was then we were better able to respect others. Thank you for that, Mama.*
>
> *To my wife, Camila, and my kids, Levi, Vida, and Mr. Stone, the courage and significance you give me every day I go out the door is unparalleled. You are the four people in my life that I want to make the proudest of me. Thank you.*
>
> *And to my hero, that's who I chase. Now when I was 15 years old, I had a very important person in my life come to me and say, "Who's your hero?" And I said, "I don't know. I gotta think about that. [. . .] You know who it is?" I said, "It's me in 10 years."*
>
> *So, I turned 25. Ten years later, that same person comes to me and goes, "So are you a hero?" And I was like, "Not even close. No, no, no." She said, "Why?" I said, "Because my hero's me at 35." [. . .]*
>
> *So, to any of us, whatever those things are, whatever it is we look up to, whatever it is we look forward to, and whoever it is we're chasing—to that I say, "Amen." To that I say, "Alright, alright, alright." To that I say, "Just keep living."*

*Lesson: The Rule of Three organizes, simplifies, and coalesces.*

## Tool No. 9: Using Your Hands

Justice Oliver Wendell Holmes famously remarked: "A word. . . is the skin of a living thought and may vary greatly in color and content according to the circumstances and the time in which it is used." He is correct.

But your words are never enough to deliver your message. For maximum impact they must be paired with your hands. Put differently, hands are an extension of your mind.

## Tell and Show

Research supports the use of hand gestures in giving effective presentations. Professor Susan Goldin-Meadow of the University of Chicago and Professor Martha Wagner Alibali of the University of Wisconsin at Madison in their article, "Gesture's Role in Speaking, Learning, and Creating Language," *Annual Rev. Psychol. 2013,* find this: Hand movements while talking are "ubiquitous" whether inadvertent or planned.

This truth spans all cultures (although some gestures are welcome in certain cultures while others condemn the same gesture). And even congenitally blind individuals—who have never seen anyone gesture—move their hands when talking!

The Professors posed this question: Do speakers' gestures affect listeners' comprehension of speech?

Yes. Across numerous research studies, the Professors find that when hand gestures express information that supplement or complement your words, they contribute to successful audience comprehension.

In controlled studies where hand gestures were prohibited, listeners' comprehension significantly decreased. The bottom line per the Professors: "When gesture is produced along with speech, it provides a second window into the speakers' thoughts, offering insight into those thoughts that cannot be found in speech [alone]."

In short, the use of your hands is baked into your DNA. Our take: While you might question whether using your hands in a presentation is natural, science tells us that it is very much so. More importantly, *your* audience is pre-wired to accept hand movements aligned with words being used.

This Tool is like tone or pacing purposefully across the stage, in that these tools are more physical in nature because they require a conscious use of your presence. As we stated in "Why Read This Book?", these are only suggested tools that you, in your judgement, decide whether to use. Because of the physical nature of this tool, we suggest you practice in front of a mirror or by recording yourself to see how you look and how you feel.

Doing so allows you to become comfortable with the Tool and to come across as natural and authentic to your audience.

The following hand gestures can be used to stress key points, transition to other topics, or help the audience members visualize the story you are telling:

***By Way of Illustration:***

- *The Frame*

Hold your hands in front of your chest, with your open palms facing each other, several inches apart. Use this at the beginning of your presentation to frame your idea or at the end to frame your conclusion.

"Today, I'm talking about a key need of our Bar." Use the hand gesture above, The Frame, and say, "To raise funds to build a new Bar Association building."

- *The Goalie*

This is a variation on the preceding hand gesture, The Frame. Instead of framing an idea, imagine holding a mini soccer ball. Hold your hands in front of your chest, with your hands cupped toward each other but still facing the other, a couple inches apart. Consider this the analogue to a bullet point when writing. It drives home a detail.

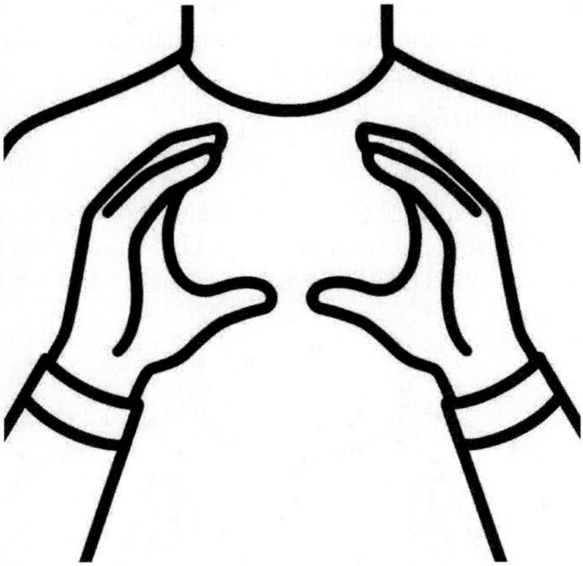

"And when you donate," Use the hand gesture above, The Goalie, and say the following: "It will result in a beautiful and functional facility for continuing legal education."

➢ *The Steeple*

Use both hands with your fingertips touching to create a church like steeple, held right below your chin. This conveys thoughtfulness and understanding. Use sparingly, generally in response to a question.

"Thanks for the insightful question." Use the hand gesture above, The Steeple, and say, "Here are my thoughts on the contemplated costs of the new building:"

➢ *The Numbers*

This is simple. When speaking about several things, consider using that number of fingers to emphasize your point. A visual image reinforcing your message helps to imprint your message into the listeners' neural pathways.

"Here are the two points that I want you to remember. . ." Raise one finger and say: "Donate." Raise two fingers and say, "And consider what you'll get, namely a commemorative plaque for your firm in the new facility." (More on this in the chapter on persuasion.)

➢ *The Accordion*

Let's say you want to use a timeline to place events into the context of time: this occurred, then this, concluding in this. Raise your hand with your palm open and stationery to anchor the start of the timeline and use your other hand with palm open parallel to the stationary one to demonstrate the next segment of time. This helps the audience sync up the timeline of the events that you create with your words with a visual image. This can also be used to stress growth. Think of the palms as endpoints and then use your non-stationary hand like an accordion, folding in and out to indicate the passage of time or growth.

While saying, "If you donate today. . ." raise your left hand, palm open, in a stationary position. While saying, "Then, in three months we can break ground," raise your right hand parallel to that stationary left hand, palm open, a couple of inches away. Then while saying "six months from now, the building will be close to completion," move that right hand further away from the stationary hand while still parallel to your hand. Finally say, "And nine months from now the building will be ready for use" and move your right hand even further from the left stationary hand.

If you're a person who uses hand gestures often and without deliberation, consider keeping your hands stationary and by your side to emphasize a central idea. This minimizes distractions and compels the audience to focus solely on your words.

*Lesson: Your hands are your friends. Use them.*

**The Neurodiversity Insight**

For many neurodivergent individuals fidgeting and stimming are physiological and neurobiological regulation tools, not external habits that can be broken. They are not things to be fixed and should not be suppressed when they serve as a coping mechanism. Consider ways of stimming/fidgeting that are not so disruptive to your audience, not because there is something wrong with you, but something to work with that acknowledges understanding of audience needs. So, incorporating a hand gesture or two (not all of them) into your regulatory tools. You can both regulate and engage your audience.

If you are comfortable doing so, consider disclosing to the audience so they do not misinterpret stimming as a nervous habit. Explain very briefly that you can't *not* do it. This demonstrates credibility and trustworthiness. For instance, one of Professor Kelly's colleagues has a benign tremor that causes her hands to shake slightly (like what a person with Parkinson's might do.) Because she knows it might be distracting to the audience—which includes clients, judges, and students—she pre-empts any misunderstanding or speculation on their part by disclosing up front.

## Tool No. 10: Using Your Voice

No matter the justness of your cause, the power of your logic, or the strength of your belief, you will lose your audience if you do not effectively use your voice. As TED Talk creator Chris Anderson said, "Give your words the life they deserve."

### Tell and Show

Here are the Four P's you can deploy: Pace, Pitch, Power, and Pause.

- **Pace**

This is your word rate—how many words you speak in a minute. Speech coach Anthony Sammi counsels that you speak at a pace close to the average pace of day-to-day conversation. This is good advice.

Beware of speaking too fast, which we've noticed is the default for many speakers. The audience does not have time to absorb what you are saying. They are simply trying to keep up with the rapid delivery. Fast talkers are not doing so consciously. Why is this so? Speakers may imagine that their audience is impatient to hear their message and thus bolt out of the gate like a racehorse and do not stop until the finish line. Time becomes distorted. How can you fix this?

**Tip No. 1: Know You Have Plenty of Time**

We assume that the audience wants to know NOW! Instead, assume positive intent on the audience's part: that they want to hear what you have to say and, if you structure the talk to their needs via the techniques we've discussed, will listen. While B.L.U.F. is a great technique as to content, it does not mean that you plunge at once into rapid fire delivery. No rush. Importantly, stating your bottom line up front, citing impactful facts, using contrast, or transforming numbers into memorable images or concepts, will electrify your audience. They need a moment to conceptualize and integrate what you are saying. Pace, repetition, and pause allow this integration to occur.

**Tip No. 2: Center Yourself Before Speaking**

This involves planting your feet firmly in one place and connecting to the ground beneath you. Take a deep breath but not an exaggerated one. Smile—not a cheesy, fake, toothy grin but a simple turning up of the lips. Control your body, control your tempo. Look at your audience, not through them. Know that the presentation will proceed one step at a time.

And a great way to center is through box breathing. Here is how it works:

- Exhale completely through your mouth
- Inhale through your nose for a count of four
- Hold your breath for a count of four
- Exhale through your mouth for a count of four
- Hold your breath for a count of four

In fact, an article in the January 17, 2023 issue of *Cell Reports Medicine* compared box breathing to other techniques for centering oneself and found it produced greater improvements to mood and reductions in respiratory rate.

**Tip No. 3: Practice Makes Perfect**

Go through your remarks, pre-delivery, and consider which words you want to stress and the emotion, hand to heart, that the stressed language triggers: serious, amused, passionate, invested, curious. Practice but do not seem to be practiced. Never memorize, be conversational. Practice makes perfect and practicing by recording yourself is a valuable self-diagnostic. Yes, we know that some readers might be self-conscious in doing do. Don't be. Programs like Zoom now integrate "Meeting Coach" tools for recordings that generate metrics with a speaker's talk-listen ratio, speed, filler words, shortest/longest spiel. Use a pen in your hand to point? Fiddle with your ring? Wear large hoop earrings? You'll more easily pick up on these distractions if you see yourself. The poet Robert Burns was so right when, in 1786 (well before smart phones) he wrote "Oh, would some Power the gift give us, to see ourselves as others see us."

***By Way of Illustration:***

President Abraham Lincoln and Union General John F. Reynolds were very close, but Reynolds was killed in action at the Battle of Gettysburg. Before giving the Gettysburg Address (after the Battle of Gettysburg), Lincoln visited the site where General Reynolds fell. Lincoln was so moved, he changed the Address, underlining where he now wanted to place stress.

> *The world will little note, nor long remember what we say here, but it can never forget what they did here. It is for us, the living, rather, to be dedicated here to the unfinished work which they who fought here have thus far so nobly advanced. It is for us, the living, rather, to be here dedicated to the great task remaining before us—that from these honored dead we take increased devotion to that cause for which they gave the* ***last full measure of devotion****—that we here highly resolve that these dead shall not have died in vain. . .*

We imagine that his voice became firmer, his pace slowed, and he enunciated more deliberately in the bolded and italicized portion above. But we know that Lincoln went back to his draft, after having visited the site where General Reynolds fell, and underlined "*last full measure of devotion.*" Lincoln honored General Reynolds by stressing this phrase. The audience very likely remembered.

- **Pitch**

Pitch is how high or low your voice sounds. Try to vary your pitch. A lower voice can be used to communicate sadness or to share somber content. We imagine President Lincoln (who reputedly had a naturally high-pitched voice) dropped a register or two when he spoke of General Reynolds. A higher pitch can be used to convey excitement or urgency. Whatever you do, do not fall into the trap of believing that only a deep and resonating voice—*a la* actors Morgan Freeman and the late James Earl Jones—is the best way to speak. Remember that effective communication is all about natural delivery, not trying to change a voice that you were born with.

- **Power**

This is also known as projection which should not be considered as volume. This is not about being loud but about being heard. Voice Coach Sammi suggests that you gauge your projection strength by stretching your arm in front of your face—at arm's length—with your palm facing you. Then try to "throw" you voice as far as your palm. In short, project your voice to arm's length. This should be sufficient to be heard.

- **Pause**

One of the most powerful tools you can use. We will return to it in the persuasion section of this book. A pause varies the timing of your presentation; you are so conversant with your material that you can forget the audience is not.

By pausing, you give the gift of time to assimilate your message. But guess what? A pause is a gift to you as well, allowing time to re-focus on where you are in the presentation and on what is coming next. It also gives you a moment to make eye contact with the audience. And most importantly, it is useful in eliminating, or at least diminishing, the distracting use of "filler words" such as "uh," "um," and "you know." Instead of filling the air with noises, reach for the pause. The bonus is that, when a pause is lengthy enough, it allows the audience to gather its attention and re-focus on the presentation. Listeners whose minds have wandered to their grocery lists or unfinished tasks will look up and reboot when you pause. What is said next should then have import as the audience is *now* listening.

***By Way of Illustration:***

Professor Maslanka teaches several substantive courses. A technique he uses, especially in the thicket of a content rich part of a lecture, is to say slowly: "Let me stress the following points because they are crucial to your understanding." He waits two beats, and then delivers the punch line. The purpose is for the class to Stop, Think, Absorb.

***By Way of Illustration:***

The poet John Keats knew the power of a pause back in 1819 when in writing his famous poem "To Autumn." Read out loud the following two versions of a section of the poem and identify the one you find more compelling:

***Option A*:**

"Where are the songs of Spring? [Pause.] Ay, where are they?

Think not of them, thou hast thy music too."

***Option B*:**

"Where are the songs of Spring?

Think not of them, thou hast thy music too."

By combining a pause with a rhetorical question, *Option A* operates to refocus the reader or the listener. We call this a cognitive breath and will re-visit the concept in the third section of this book. Check out Professor Maslanka's video. https://bit.ly/persuasionandpoetry.

*Lesson: Be holistic.*

**The Neurodiversity Insight**

Neurodivergent and neurotypical individuals tend to perceive pace, tone, and pause differently which can lead to miscommunication and misunderstanding.

So, what should a neurotypical communicator do? Start by acknowledging that people are different and have different communication styles. Try to understand where the person is coming from instead of jumping to conclusions or making assumptions.

And what should the neurodivergent communicator do? Understand that you may speak at a quick pace, but that trying to slow down—especially one on one—might come across as inadvertently patronizing. So, while you should pay attention to your speed, focus more on your pacing by adding pauses. This gives a neurodivergent person time to process their environment and stimuli, making for a more effective presentation.

## Tool No. 11: Using Your Body

We've gone over using your voice and hands as tools to convey your message. Likewise, your body is a powerful tool for communication.

### Tell and Show

Avoid low powered poses. These involve turning away your body or face away from the audience while speaking. Or perhaps crossing your arms or lowering your head. Such actions, like locking your hands in front of you in a fig leaf position or hunching your shoulders, signals to others that you have something to hide. By using these low powered poses or physically shrinking into oneself, speakers can unconsciously convey that they don't believe what they are saying or cannot be trusted: An unintended vibe to be avoided.

But how? What we create we can undo. Speaking Coach Dr. Amy Cuddy suggests the use of high-powered poses before making a presentation, being interviewed for a job, and other nerve-wracking activity. Try, for instance, standing with your feet firmly planted and apart, standing tall with your chin up before your audience, with your hands on your hips.

How else can the body be used? A speaker can mark the passage of time in a narrative, or a transition of thoughts in the presentation, by walking across the stage. Sorrow, regret, and solemnity can be underscored through a slightly bowed head, while humor can be conveyed with a head tilt or upward shrug.

Two of the authors of this book love dogs, maybe to excess. And having bonded with more than a few dogs in their lifetime, these authors know something you may know as well. Dogs and people communicate quite well through physical posture and movement. Putting on your shoes and stretching? Your dog may fetch the leash for the impending jog in the park. Sitting slumped and sighing deeply? Your dog may snuggle up and offer attention.

But people communicate quite well with one another too, through gestures and body language. This is especially true in the context of deposition or trial, where visual distractions are limited, the focus of those present is on the participants, and the smallest details come under scrutiny.

The effective communicator is conscious of the many ways in which posture, gesture, movement, and physical presence convey meaning. Bringing non-verbal messaging in line with the words spoken conveys trustworthiness and credibility and reinforces the message. Let's get ahead of ourselves for a minute and talk about four illustrations that fit nicely on the chapter of persuading.

***By Way of Illustration:***

Consider a trial in which attorney and client sit at some distance from one another, turn their bodies away from one another, and do not interact. A fair takeaway for the courtroom observer might be that the attorney does not believe in their client's case, or that the client does not believe or endorse the argument of their counsel. Credibility is lost, and possibly also the case. An alternative approach is to sit closer to the client, lean in to speak with them, turn your body towards them, sometimes touch their shoulder or elbow when speaking. With your body language you are communicating an interest and belief in your client's position. The same technique can be useful at deposition.

***By Way of Illustration:***

Confidence in one's legal position and/or the credibility of one's client can be conveyed non-verbally throughout the trial process. A calm body, a steady tone, eye contact, the omission of filler words such as "um" and "you know," and the avoidance of restless or redundant hand gestures, all convey that the presenter knows what they are talking about and is confident that they are correct. These non-verbal signals trigger confidence in the audience, whether judge or jury. They give assurance that the speaker is truthful, knowledgeable, and sincere.

***By Way of Illustration:***

So, what should the presenting attorney try not to do, with non-verbal cues? If at a podium, the presenting attorney should avoid the white-knuckled grip on the sides of the podium, as it indicates nervousness, and may cause the listener to believe the speaker does not have confidence in what they are saying. The same can be true when an attorney rocks in their chair at counsel table or bounces their knees up and down. Movements like these can be interpreted as nervousness, and a lack of confidence—thus calling into question the counsel's credibility.

***By Way of Illustration:***

Our clients should also be advised about body language, and the importance of their physical and verbal behavior while in and near the courthouse (such as in the parking garage). One never knows who is watching. An example is the Plaintiff in a legal malpractice case defended years ago by one of this book's authors, Professor LeBoeuf.

The underlying case was medical malpractice, and the Plaintiff claimed the underlying case was lost for failure by her counsel to obtain an appropriate medical expert. To win at trial, Plaintiff had to prove that she would have won the underlying case—for which she had hoped to obtain damages for physical injury—had her attorney not provided services that fell below the standard of care. Plaintiff did not attend the legal malpractice trial, from day to day. In fact, her attorney told the venire members during voir dire that Plaintiff had a brain injury (made the subject of the underlying case) and could not sit and participate in a trial. Plaintiff did, however, appear for testimony at the trial.

On the stand, she barely spoke above a whisper and asked repeatedly for clarification of the questions asked. She hunched her shoulders and seemed to shrink into her chair throughout the questioning. On lunch break, however, she was in the hallway telling jokes with her sister, laughing, and walking around with her head high and shoulders back. Unfortunately for this plaintiff, at this very moment the jurors were filing by a glass door at the end of the hallway, headed to lunch. They were astonished to see the Plaintiff appearing both confident and healthy, very different from how she appeared on the stand. While the jurors could not hear her words, Plaintiff's body language (and especially her radical transformation between the witness stand and the hallway) conveyed an important message: that she could not be trusted. Plaintiff did not prevail in her case.

*Lesson: Be aware. People watch your body before they hear your words.*

**The Neurodiversity Insight**

Neurotypical and neurodivergent individuals struggle to understand each other's communication styles because each uses body language differently, which can lead to miscommunication and misunderstanding. In the "Double Empathy Theory" developed by sociologist and social psychologist Dr. Damian Milton, the idea is advanced that miscommunication and misunderstandings are not the fault of neurotypical individuals or the fault of neurodivergent individuals. They stem from a lack of understanding between people who experience the world differently.

Because neurodivergent individuals process information differently than neurotypical individuals, they tend to rely less on neurotypical facial expressions, voice tone and body language. For example, when it comes to listening, some neurodivergent individuals focus better by gazing or looking away. If you didn't know this, you might think the person is not listening or not engaged. A neurodivergent person may cross their arms when speaking because it keeps them from moving them all around (which is distracting). If you didn't know this, you might think the person is closed off or defensive. Effective communication is when the speaker and the audience demonstrate respect for each other. It means being cognizant of us and others and not jumping to conclusions when someone is different.

We need to communicate with our clients about body language and non-verbal cues and do it in a way that respects the individual, acknowledges there can be disconnects in communication styles, and gives them the agency to decide what they want to do. For example, if your client shifts back and forth as a way to self-regulate, your instinct might be to tell them to stop. This approach treats neurodivergence as a problem that needs to be fixed, and the only solution is to mask. Sometimes people think masking might be okay in small doses. It is not. Even if a neurodivergent person is "good" at masking, it will negatively impact their ability to focus, listen, participate. Remember, masking is not a nervous habit that you can "untrain" yourself from doing. It requires constant suppression. Consider how you would feel if there was a fly buzzing right by your ear and you could not acknowledge it in any way. Neurotypical communication styles are not better (or worse) than neurodivergent. The better approach comes back to respecting the individual while acknowledging the disconnect in communication styles and giving the client the agency to decide what they want to do:

"I noticed you tend to rock a bit during mediation, and it could be because you are nervous, or it is how you stay regulated. This can sometimes be perceived as nervous and that you have something to hide, which I know is not the case. If this is how you regulate, I can explain that, or you can. If you would prefer not to disclose this, we can come up with something that works for you."

The above example should not be used verbatim, but it shows how we can support decision-making and represents an important concept in the disability community called, "the dignity of making bad decisions" which is about self-determination. This right to make decisions is a given for many of us and includes both good and bad, whether it is eating Hot Cheetos for breakfast or wearing uncomfortable but cute shoes and getting a blister We know the risks associated and it is our decision. The same is true here.

**FINDING YOUR VOICE**

Pick a poem: it can be a favorite poem from college, a new poet you recently discovered, or a poem you found online while randomly searching. Pick an audience: your colleague, roommate, partner, neighbor, cousin. Read the poem through once out loud and ask your audience what they heard. What was the poem about? How does it make them feel? Now read it out loud again but this time utilize some of the tools in this Challenge: change the pace, use pauses to gather attention and augment meaning, vary your tone, repeat a line, use your hands. *Now*, ask your audience what they heard. Notice how delivery changes the responses.

## III. CONCLUDING

### The Challenge: How Do I End a Presentation?

Your start is engaging. The good vibe trajectory continues. Now, time to wrap up. Audience attention is high again, so end strongly. Sports fans may liken this to pushing into the end zone; scoring a goal; or, slapping the puck into the net.

### Tool No. 1: Know What Not to Say

Here is a list of conventional but ineffective closes:

- "Well, that just about covers it. Thank you!"
- "I see I am out of time."
- "That does it. Any questions?"
- "Let me summarize what I promised to tell you and what I told you."

Each a potential close, each equally ineffective. To borrow a phrase, they each end "not with a bang, but with a whimper." *T.S. Eliot, The Hollow Men, in Collected Poems, 1909–1962 89 (Harcourt, Brace & World, 1st ed. 1963).*

## Tool No. 2: Foreshadow the Close

To ensure the audience is focused on the message that you want to deliver, foreshadow the close. Tell the audience, "I am about to wrap up." If otherwise, it's all just one stream of information without any demarcation and is harder to follow and to give sustained engagement. This Tool is a form of buffering that we discussed earlier.

## Tell and Show

Let's go back to our chart:

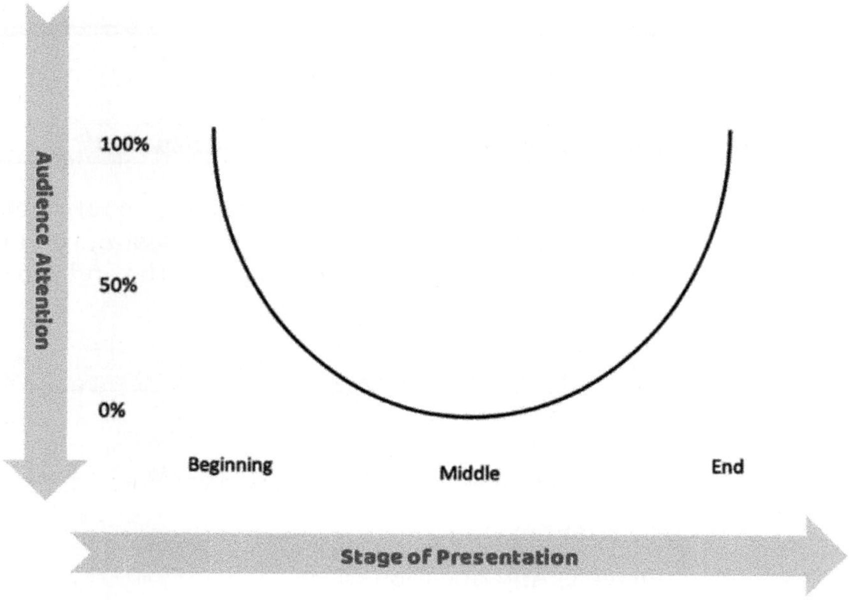


Notice that the level of audience engagement/attention rises at the end of the presentation. But it does not do so naturally. The speaker needs to tee up the audience, letting them know that the end is coming. Otherwise, the rising slope between "Middle" and "End" does not rise as you see in the chart, it "flat lines."

When you foreshadow, a neurotransmitter called dopamine is released into the brains of the audience members sending messages between our nerve cells and the rest of our body. You may have heard it referred to as the "feel-good chemical" because it is involved in several functions of pleasure and satisfaction.

Other reactions?

- Reward system is activated
- Learning activity/emotional responses are enhanced
- Focus is narrowed

How is dopamine released? By anticipation.

### *The Spotlight*

Enter President Lincoln and his first inaugural address in 1861. His key message was "let us not go to war" (yes, it did not work but not for lack of rhetorical skill). He very likely intuitively knew that he needed a signpost to let the audience know he was nearing the close. All of the above would be triggered. Here is President Lincoln giving a shot of dopamine:

> *I am loathe to close. We are not enemies, but friends. We must not be enemies. Though passion may have strained it must not break our bonds of affection. The mystic chords of memory, stretching from every battlefield and patriot grave to every living heart and hearthstone all over this broad land, will yet swell the chorus of the Union, when again touched, as surely they will be, by the better angels of our nature.*

The signpost of "I am loathe to close" was genius, signaling that he is near done. It is genius. It is also portable to all types of presentations. Our brains work the same now as they did in 1861.

*Lesson: Dopamine, get some.*

## Tool No. 3: Making Takeaway Points Memorable

Let's talk about what this tool is *not* about: repeating what you have said in the body of the presentation. It is more than summarizing what you just said. To merely summarize is pointless repetition, not actionable enlightenment. Rather, this Tool is about distilling the body of the talk, lightening the cognitive load of the audience members. Put differently, highlighting/naming/spotlighting the messages you want the audience members to walk away with.

### Tell and Show

Back to psychologist George A. Miller who also made a groundbreaking discovery about the limits of human consciousness. Miller found that, at most, we can only hold seven units of information at any one time. But the brain prefers these units packaged in a concise, relevant, streamlined format. This is the purpose of this Tool.

There are various ways to deliver the takeaway points. Think back to our Tool on the Power of Three. As Daniel Ramirez writes in "What is the Mysterious Rule of Three?" history proves the effectiveness of the Rule as a way for audience members (or readers) to encode a speaker's message.

Look at the close of the Declaration of Independence:

"Our lives, our fortunes, our sacred honor."

Or consider the close to the Gettysburg Address:

"(That) government of the people, by the people, for the people shall not perish from the earth."

*Lesson: Your final words are often your most critical words.*

## Tool No. 4: A Call to Action's Primary Purpose

A Call to Action is an effective way to close a presentation. It can be as simple as asking the audience to follow you on social media or as elevated as donating money or as lofty as asking the nation to go to war or discard years of racial segregation.

## Tell and Show

Its primary purpose is to change a listener from a passive observer to an active participant; to seek alignment between the audience and the speaker's goals.

There are two types: Direct Call to Action and Informational Call to Action. The first specifically invites a person to take a specific immediate action. The second specifically invites the listener to discover more about your idea or campaign before taking any action. Whatever your call to action, it must be Clear, Concise, and Actionable.

Here are tips in constructing a Call to Action:

- Understand the audience. Know whether they would be receptive to the message. Ask: what is in it for them?
- Define your goal. Only then can you measure whether your talk was a success.
- Use actionable language. Deploy verbs. "join" or "explore" or "inquire".
- Create urgency. This translates into prompt action.
- Be clear and concise. Why? The goal is for the listener to immediately grasp what you are asking them to do. Skip filler language, avoid white noise, omit distracting details.

### *The Spotlight*

Let's return to Hubert Humphrey and the 1948 Democratic Convention. He is asking for the delegates to vote for the civil rights platform.

> *[. . .] My good friends, I ask my party, the Democratic Party, to march down the high road of progressive democracy. I ask this convention to say, in unmistakable terms, that we proudly hail and courageously support our President and leader, Harry Truman, in his great fight for civil rights in America!*

What makes this so powerful? There is no misunderstanding of what he wants or why he wants it. For a more complete discussion of this talk, check out Professor Maslanka's video: https://bit.ly/calltoactionmpm.

Here is Winston Churchill asking his nation to win a war. Consider Churchill's effective use of the rule of three, coupled with the framing tool of the rhetorical question, in his famous "blood, sweat and tears" speech to the British House of Commons on the eve of the breakout of World War II. As you read this, consider how Churchill used these techniques.

> *You ask, what is our policy? It is to wage war by sea, land, and air with all our might and with all the strength that God can give us to wage war [. . .] that is our policy.*
>
> *You ask, what is our aim? I can answer in one word: it is victory. Victory at all costs. Victory despite all terror. Victory however hard and long the road may be [. . .] for without victory there is no survival for the British Empire, no survival for all that the British Empire has stood for. No survival for the urge and impulse of the ages, that mankind will move forward towards its goal.*

**The Neurodiversity Insight**

Let's pause for a minute to discuss an issue permeating this Section and flowing into the next Section (Counseling); namely, disclosure by a neurodivergent lawyer whether dealing with ADHD, autism, Tourette's Syndrome or similar conditions. These conditions can be accompanied by physical manifestations that are noticeable to others.

We recognize that disclosing a condition or a disability can be a deeply personal and private decision. It is not easy to disclose something that others—especially prospective clients, ongoing clients, witnesses, audience members, judges, students—might misunderstand. You must weigh the benefits of being your authentic self against these costs. These benefits include gaining credibility and instilling trustworthiness. If you elect disclosure, here are some how-to tips:

Very briefly say that you can't *not* engage in these manifestations—rocking in a chair, bouncing knees, uncontrollable tremors. Transparency gets you points. Informing others should take on a matter-of-fact tone.

"You may notice that my hand trembles. I have Parkinson's, and I've learned that it is just easier to mention it rather than have you guess." (Both Professors Kelly and Maslanka know individuals who do so.)Finally, when you do so, you place your client's need for understanding of your situation above your need for privacy. That is the very definition of a professional.

*Lesson: Lead by giving the audience a reason to follow you.*

**FINDING YOUR VOICE**

Let's say that you are giving the talk about the gift campaign raising money for the new bar building in your city. Using one or several of the Tools discussed in this Challenge, write a close using the facts below:

- The bar building is a historic building in your city. It serves as a hub for local lawyers. The last renovation took place 23 years ago and both the physical condition and functionality of the building are outdated. A number of attorneys expressed their concerns at the last Continuing Legal Education (CLE) presentation. Additionally, while the bar building is booking weddings, the outdated facilities impact the bar's ability to sell the space.
- Consider a recent debate with a friend, colleague, or family member. Maybe you were discussing the best way to approach a client problem or a team project. Maybe you were debating a current event. Write the closing for the position you've taken. What is your call to

action? Frame it in a way that matters to the person with whom you conversed. Use the Power of Three.

CHAPTER 2

# COUNSELING

Communication challenges permeate counseling. And here understand that "communication" is an expansive concept, encompassing not only words that are said but also unsaid, actions that are done but also not done, gestures that are made but also not made. Rule 1.4 in the Model Rules of Professional Conduct ("Model Rules") is devoted entirely to Communication.

We will see this proposition in a variety of areas-forming or not an attorney-client relationship, finding clients in the first place, interviewing clients and, ultimately, doing what only lawyers can do on legal matters—counsel, advise, care.

And there is a consequence to ineffective communication: lawyer grievances. The State Bar of Texas published enlightening grievance-made statistics from the earlier part of this decade. Here is the breakdown:

- 28% Poor or no communication.
- 24% Lack of integrity
- 5% Neglect
- 14% Declining or terminating representation

ABA statistics confirm these numbers. Keep that 28% in mind as you read through this section. Consider how you have communicated and how you could have done a better job. But *also* consider the times when you communicated effectively, how good it felt for you, and how you can replicate that rewarding feeling.

## I. ATTORNEY-CLIENT RELATIONSHIP FORMATION (OR NOT)

### The Challenge: How Do I Find a Client?

Someone decides whether to hire you based on what you communicate about yourself and how you communicate it. This is a matter of both professional ethics and effective advocacy.

The following Tools will help you navigate this sometimes-challenging dichotomy.

## Tool No. 1: Be Honest About Yourself

Talking about yourself may manifest itself in many forms—billboards, social media posts, television or radio messages, one-on-one communication. While these are diverse communication mediums, they each share a single value: You must be honest about your skills, your background, and your promises.

### Tell and Show

Here's a red alert for you: While this is a Tool, honesty is also mandated by the ethical rules governing lawyers.

Lawyer communication with prospective clients is largely governed by provisions in the Model Rules as adopted by each state. The Model Rules on lawyer communication are based on a common sense understanding of human nature, namely: Each of us believes we are more honest than reality allows.

This is all too human, and this is why Model Rule 7.1 (Communication Concerning a Lawyer's Services) provides guardrails for lawyers in terms of selling themselves. It prohibits "false or misleading" communication.

***By Way of Illustration:***

Let us make our point by reverting to the childhood fable of Goldilocks and the Three Bears:

You're a second-year associate with one trial win under your belt. How should you communicate to a prospective client your trial abilities:

**Too Much:** "I have never lost a trial!"

If the lawyer has only tried one or a handful of cases, then this statement is misleading.

**Too Little:** "I will try your case."

This is ineffective advocacy because it provides too little information.

**Just right:** "I will try your case based on my two years of litigation experience, including one trial to a jury. And I work closely with a Senior Partner in trying all of my cases as well."

It's factually honest and it provides the prospective client with the necessary information to start on the path to making an informed decision.

*Lesson: Here's Mark Twain: "Always tell the truth. That way, you don't have to remember what you said." Good advice.*

**The Neurodiversity Insight**

At the end of the last section, we discussed neurodivergent disclosure to audiences when giving a presentation. Human nature is such that the overwhelming number of people in an audience want you to do well, whether the speaker is neurotypical or neurodivergent. Their self-interested goal is to learn or to be educated or to decide, so they care about understanding the material. Period. By the same metric, prospective clients/actual clients come to lawyers to fix something that they cannot fix themselves. They are looking for answers/solutions/options. Period. Being neurodivergent is unrelated to those goals. Indeed, self-disclosure adds to your credibility and does not diminish it.

## Tool No. 2: Ask for Business

The easiest way to get business is asking for business. Simple communication? Normally yes but as a profession our communications are regulated by our ethical duties. Why these guardrails?

### Tell and Show

Some points to keep in mind:

- The unrestricted right of the public to hire the lawyer of their choice

This is a fundamental ethical precept. It is about the client's issues and concerns, not ours, and therefore they should be able to select the lawyer who (in their view) best suits the matters at hand.

➢ A Fair Selection Process

Lawyers are trained persuaders and advocates for others. Prospective clients are not. It is hard to switch off those skills when seeking business for ourselves. So, the solicitation process is inherently an unfair fight.

➢ A Public Profession

We serve the public. So, how the public perceives us matters, and it matters a lot. Trust in a lawyer does not begin when a lawyer is hired, it begins before the lawyer is hired. Check out this clip from the movie The Rainmaker, on communicating with a prospective client in his hospital bed. Consider how the lawyer went too far and why we have the solicitation rules. Here's the link: https://bit.ly/4oOzaJF.

***Solicitation Checklist***

☑ Am I seeking business from a person in a live person-to-person context?

☑ If so, STOP unless it involves one of the following scenarios:

  ☒ Am I seeking business from a person, but my main motive is not monetary gain? (Example: providing a greatly reduced rate to a friend)

  ☒ Am I soliciting a fellow lawyer? (OK because you are both trained persuaders)

  ☒ Am I soliciting a family member, close personal friend, or person/entity with whom I have had a prior business or professional relationship and doing so without duress/coercion? (OK because there is a prior interaction and thus solicitation can be expected by the person solicited; there is no threat of damage to public image of the profession except for the one bite rule: if they say "NO" once, then further direct solicitation is a violation.)

*Lesson: Don't take advantage.*

## Tool No. 3: Practice Your Elevator Pitch

The art of communication is translating complex concepts into simple terms. Enter the concept of an elevator pitch which we define as a concise, memorable summary typically lasting 30 to 60 seconds (the length of an elevator ride) describing who you are, what you do, and—most importantly—why it matters. (Note that Model Rule 7.1 is still operative).

### Tell and Show

You are at the holiday party of your spouse. Or perhaps at a mixer at your church. Or maybe waiting for the condo association meeting to start. Someone asks you: "So, what do you do?" Compare the following two elevator pitches:

***Option A*:**

Lawyer: "I practice labor and employment law at a mid-sized firm. I really enjoy it. Been doing it for almost 3 years now."

Response: Glazed over eyes. A polite nod. Glancing around for another to talk with.

*Option A* provides no entry point for a conversation.

***Option B*:**

Lawyer: "I am an employment lawyer representing tech companies. I really enjoy it. It gives me the opportunity to deal with entrepreneurs personally; the area is also intellectually stimulating."

Response: Why do you enjoy it? What types of entrepreneurs? How is it intellectually stimulating? Which option is more likely to prompt a question or a follow-up from the questioner?

See how *Option B is* target rich with possible follow-ups.

An elevator pitch's purpose is *not* merely to convey information but to also prompt questions from the person you are speaking to. From one question can come a conversation, and from one conversation can come the start of a relationship. From a relationship can come a case.

*Lesson: Practice your elevator pitch so that it doesn't seem rehearsed.*

## Tool No. 4: Be More than Just a Lawyer

When you are seeking clients (or dealing with a current client) you will not be talking law 24/7. Be a well-educated person (not just a well-educated and knowledgeable lawyer), an engaged citizen, a good friend to others, and/or an involved parent. Communication encompasses more than just communicating about the law in legal settings. Much more.

### Tell and Show

- Professor LeBoeuf suggests broadening your base of communication contacts. These communication communities might be found in a church, synagogue or mosque, in service organizations, in communities of hobbyists or gamers, through participation in sports or outdoor activities (e.g., a rock-climbing gym or adult soccer team), and yes in clubs and participation in local, state, or national bar committees. In short: be involved.
- Professor Maslanka suggests that you read. It can be the local newspaper, the New York Times, the Washington Post, the Wall Street Journal, the Harvard Business Review, Cosmopolitan. Or that you watch. This can involve anything from YouTube and Tik Tok videos to a documentary on Netflix. In short: be informed.
- Professor Kelly suggests that you develop your professional network by developing yourself as a whole person because communicating that you are a lawyer is too limiting a message. Lawyering is your job, not your identity. Her actions are a form of communication—starting twenty years ago as a volunteer at a Special Olympics swim meet, then becoming a coach in multiple sports, and now her current role as a member of the Board of Directors

for an organization supporting individuals with intellectual disabilities. In short, be caring.

*Lesson: Know there is a world beyond your world.*

**The Neurodiversity Insight**

The brain can only take in and hold so much information, and even someone with the strongest auditory processing skills can get overwhelmed when faced with too much information. Hone your elevator pitch and make it accessible to the most people, instead of tailoring it to the "average" person. Make a list of everything you think/need to say, then categorize it into 2–3 concepts. Next, get rid of everything that is not necessary to a basic understanding of those points. Just because you know every detail and nuance, does not mean you need to cram it into your elevator pitch or the initial consultation. We've all been in classes, CLEs, presentations that seem to go on forever because the speaker was bogged down in the minutiae. Shift your thinking from, "what is everything they need to know," to "what are the three key things they need to know."

**FINDING YOUR VOICE**

Think about the area of law you like best. Write a short elevator pitch that identifies this area of practice and your interest in representing clients in this practice area. Demonstrate your enthusiasm by the words you choose. For added bonus points, credential yourself in the pitch, by establishing your interest, experience, or pursuit of this area of law by use of a short reference (e.g., "which is an interest I developed while studying under. . .") or story (e.g., "as I learned while finding the solution to a client's recent dilemma regarding. . ."). Practice your delivery with a colleague or friend.

## Tool No. 5: Rejecting a Prospective Client

Rejection is a loaded word. It feels bad. With empathy, we feel bad for those we reject. Somewhere along the line, we have all been rejected, and we know it can be surprising, hurtful, shameful even. And yet rejection is a fact of legal life. Many calls come in, while a relative handful of prospective clients are chosen. So, what do we do with this? How do we handle turning someone away? What communication skills can we take into this act of saying no?

### Tell and Show

Setting aside conflicts that may exist, where the explanation is very straightforward, we can think about the rejection of prospective clients as falling into three tiers:

(1) Outside the scope (not the right practice area, beyond the current bandwidth, outside the geographic area, court, or other type of venue in which we intend to practice);

(2) The Goldilocks problem (too big or too small versus just right); and

(3) Not a good fit (conflicts, differing personalities, goals, policy interests, etc.).

For each of these categories, the handling of prospective clients is much the same.

*First*, see the person behind the problem. Everybody wants to be seen and acknowledged. A simple recognition of the present predicament is communication at the human level. Affirmations such as, "that sounds very hard for you" or "I'm sorry you're experiencing this right now" can provide a little relief to a person who, probably, never thought they'd be dialing a stranger to ask for professional help.

*Second*, acknowledge clearly that you cannot undertake the representation. Being clear and direct frees the potential client to look for help elsewhere. Words like "You have a good case, but I'm not sure this is a good fit" or "We'd really like to help, but it would be better if you try somewhere else" are confusing. The prospective client will probably hear the first half of the sentence more clearly than the second. Stating simply that you cannot take the matter is clear, positive, and direct. You do not need to give a reason. In fact, much of the time the reason is not helpful. Whatever you do, avoid making up a reason. People value honesty and directness. Stating that you are too busy to take a new matter, for instance, is (1) probably not true; and (2) likely to have unintended consequences like discouraging a future referral.

*Third*, thank the prospective client with words, and maybe action, for thinking of you and seeking your help. It is important to do this only after making the very clear statement that you will not take the matter. Words like, "I very much appreciate your consideration of us and wish you well," leave a door open for future work and/or future referrals. The optional action step is to then follow the thank you with a referral to another lawyer, firm, or organization.

Being helpful in this way underscores your message to the potential client that they are seen and heard, and that you value their connection with you, however brief. It is an optional step, however, because you should only make referrals when you feel the potential client has a viable matter, and when you can truly recommend the place to which you are making the referral. Anything less, and the effort is likely to backfire. No lawyer likes to receive a referral from someone who has no clear claims, or who behaves badly towards staff.

There will be potential clients referred by former clients, friends, family, colleagues, that you just cannot accept as a client. Honoring the source of the referral is encompassed in the above steps, although it equally honors the potential client who calls out of the blue, with no referral.

*Fourth*, rejection takes practice, because it requires a full stop. When we feel bad, or feel empathy, we may be tempted to provide more. More explanations. More helpful advice. The problem with advising anyone you are not taking as a client is that it is confusing to the potential client. Do you or don't you represent them? Just saying you do not represent someone does not avoid a sticky situation, if you are also providing advice.

And advising about the strength of a potential matter, the length of potentially applicable limitations periods, or the potential damages available, for instance, can cross a line that puts you in the position of possibly being held liable if you are wrong. And of course you may be wrong in your advice, precisely because you do not have all of the information and have not undertaken representation, with all that it entails.

***By Way of Illustration:***

Here is a dilemma for all lawyers:

As the first lawyer in your family/circle of friends, when someone says, "I need a lawyer" your proud (and well meaning) family and friends will say, "I know one!" The result is a phone call from Janine, your aunt's neighbor's friend from book club, who needs legal help in updating her will. Except you are developing a criminal defense practice. What to do?

- Create a network of lawyers from various specialties by attending bar events, CLE presentations, community activities, law alumni events. Refer Janine to a trusts, wills, and estate lawyer. And guess what? You now have a node in your network who may refer a DWI case to you.
- Leverage their pride by educating them on the various and numerous specialties there are in the law, just like doctors! The civilian population (i.e. non-lawyer) believes that once admitted to the bar you become, abracadabra, an expert in all things legal. So, take the obstacle and convert it to a benefit by arming family/friends so they can proselytize for you. Ensure your aunt can repeat your specialty to others.
- Remember your first duty as a lawyer is being competent in matters that you undertake per Model Rule 1.1. Communicate this as well to family/ friends. It is an appropriate explanation for why you cannot take certain types of matters.

*Lesson: Saying "No" is more than okay.*

## Tool No. 6: Send a Non-Engagement Communication

Every "No" to a prospective client does not warrant a follow up communication. But, when a follow-up is warranted, you should have a set formula for what you include and what you do not include.

### Tell and Show

You should always send a follow-up communication when prospective clients state they have an immediate or pressing deadline or need. By Way of Example, when they have received a notice of foreclosure, or are nearing a limitations deadline (or when their explanation of the facts make that seem likely), or when there is an impending hearing or trial. Moreover, if you decide you will not be taking on a matter, do not procrastinate in letting the person know there will be no formation of an attorney-client relationship ("ACR"). For non-lawyers, a prolonged length of time after an initial consultation may lead them to believe that you have already taken on their matter. Don't presume otherwise.

***By Way of Illustration:***

Here is language ***not*** to include:

- "If you have any questions, please call us." The non-engagement communication missive should leave no doubt that there will be no ACR. Do not leave the door open for any other interpretation or communication.

- "While you arguably have a viable claim, we are not interested in representing you at this time." As with the bullet above, this is polite, and we are raised to be polite. But offering a legal opinion on a matter is the essence of ACR creation.

- "Thank you for meeting with us on your claim of sexual harassment." Yes, the prospective client might have characterized their claim, but by agreeing with the characterization you are yet again offering a legal opinion.

***By Way of Illustration:***

Here is the language ***to*** include:

- "Our decision not to represent you should not be taken as an opinion on whether you have a valid claim." In effective communication, the more something goes without saying, the more it needs to be said.
- "We urge you to seek other counsel as soon as possible because each potential claim has a statute of limitations which means that it must be brought within a certain period of time or be lost." Or, "There are time limitations for responding to filed claims, and you should not delay in securing counsel." Note that this is not legal advice because it only offers generic counsel, not counsel specific to an individual, such as stating there is a three-year statute of limitations
- "We wish you well."

Also important in a final communication to prospective clients: tell them their communications with you are privileged and explain that this means they are private. Others cannot find out what the two of you talked about or even that you did talk. This is especially important to tell a prospective client if you cannot take their case because of conflict or potential conflict.

*Lesson: If your rejection is not in writing, then the rejection does not exist.*

## The Challenge: How Do I Start an ACR?

What ends well, starts well. And here is your chance to get off on the right note through honest, direct, and candid communication.

## Tool No. 1: Understand the Parameters of an ACR

As with solicitation, so too with ACR formation: the ethical rules define the ballpark you will play in.

## Tell and Show

Statistically, only a small percentage of lawyers are disciplined for ethical rule violations, but that does not mean you will not encounter ethical dilemmas.

No one enters the legal profession thinking they will act unethically or violate the Model Rules. Law school Professional Responsibility course(s) focus on what these rules are and the importance of complying with them. It is hard for students to imagine themselves engaging in unethical practices, and yes, while the rules might seem clear when learned individually in a classroom environment, it is more complicated in practice. So much so that the Preamble to the Model Rules acknowledges that "difficult ethical issues" can arise because of potentially conflicting rules associated with client obligations.

***By Way of Illustration:***

Let's look at the tension between MR 1.2 and MR 3.1: MR 1.2 says in pertinent part that "a lawyer shall abide by a client's decisions concerning the objectives of representation. . ." and Comment 1 explains that this "confers upon the client the ultimate authority to determine the purposes to be served by legal representation, within the limits imposed by law and the lawyer's professional obligations."

MR 3.1 says, "[a] lawyer shall not bring or defend a proceeding, or assert or controvert an issue therein, unless there is a basis in law and fact for doing so that is not frivolous. . ." Comment 1 explains that, "[t]he advocate has a duty to use legal procedure for the fullest benefit of the client's cause, but also a duty not to abuse legal procedure."

So, while MR 1.2 makes clear that the client is the ultimate authority to determine the purpose of representation and requires an attorney to abide by their client's wishes, MR 3.1 imposes a limit on that "ultimate" authority. The client is not your "boss" in the sense that they control the manner and means of representation such as making tactical decisions and dictating strategic steps. Recognizing and acknowledging this tension is the starting point for managing client expectations and competently navigating the course of the relationship, adjusting as necessary to be sure you have the same understanding of the goals of representation.

*Lesson: An ACR is like any other business deal. Treat it that way.*

## Tool No. 2: Establish Your Boundaries

Professional salespeople say that "the best sale they make is the sale they did not make." Never be so desperate for business that you skip over communicating your boundaries." What you stand for and what you can't stand, as the saying goes.

### Tell and Show

Here are three scenarios of communicating a boundary:

*Scenario No. 1*: The Case of the Ethically Dubious Client Request

This is a true story with a few facts changed to make sure it remains anonymous. You are working with a client to draft their will. The client is divorced and has two school-age children. The client has a few family heirlooms he wants to leave to his children, an antique firearm and his great grandfather's pocket watch. You discuss with him how to decide which item he wants to leave to each child. He says he also has something he wants to leave to his ex-wife. . . his lower intestine. At first you are confused and think maybe it's some type of organ donation. You ask and he says he wants to leave it to her because it's full of baloney, just like her. He knows she won't actually get it, but he wants her to know how he feels.

This is not illegal, and it is not a crime, and it may not violate the Model Rules, but whether you agree to include it is ethically questionable. What do you do?

Acknowledge that your obligation to him as your client is to preserve his wishes. Discuss the reasons for doing this and articulate how this does (or does not) align with his values and ultimate goals. Explain the impacts of putting this in the will—it will not be carried out, but it might also give rise to questions about other bequests, like the family heirlooms he wants his children to have. If he is vindictive in the will, it gives his ex-wife ammunition to be vindictive and there won't be anything he can do about it because he is gone. What will his children think of him, regardless of what their relationship is with their mother? This will certainly impact his legacy and what they remember of him.

In this scenario, the client ultimately agreed that it was not a mature or responsible thing to do. He did not care about his ex-wife, but he cared about his children and ultimately that is what influenced his decision. But what if the client insisted he still wanted to include the provision? The client might determine goals, but you advise and counsel how best to achieve those goals. This is where it is critical to be forthright and honest—explain why this is not something you are willing to include in the will because it reflects on your professional reputation. The client might not care what others think, but you do and including a provision like this in the will shows poor professional taste. Your professional identity is one of integrity, honesty, respect.

*Scenario No. 2*: The Case of the Rubber-Stamping Lawyer

> Omar is a real estate lawyer and is asked by a new client to help her buy a house in the Bahamas. Omar agrees to the representation. He looks up the house on a specialized website and sees that it is essentially a dilapidated shack. The client then tells Omar that she will be paying $500,000 for the house. Omar is shocked and tells her the purchase price is way out of proportion to the house's value. The client says, "Oh, don't worry, I have a good eye."

Omar suspects money laundering but does as requested because he must "abide" by the client's objective, which is buying the house. Not so fast, says the American Bar Association in Formal Opinion 513. (August 23, 2024).

Communication is not just telling but also *asking*. Here, this duty requires Omar to drill down into whether this is a money laundering scheme or just bad judgment. The Opinion is clear:

> [L]awyers must conduct a reasonable inquiry and assessment, proportionate to the risks presented by the facts and circumstances . . . when the lawyer's inquiry leaves the lawyer with unresolved questions of fact

> about whether the current or prospective client seeks to use or persists on using the lawyer's services to commit or further a crime or fraud. The lawyer must make additional efforts to resolve those questions through further reasonable inquiry proportionate to the risks, so that the lawyer may reduce the risk of counseling or assisting in a crime or fraud.

In short: you may not adopt an ostrich-like attitude of self-delusion by sticking your head in the sand. You must ask questions, such as:

- How did you learn of this opportunity?
- Have you done business before with the seller?
- What do you know about the seller?
- Why do you specifically believe this is a good investment?
- Why are you doing this business with person or entity in a foreign country? Footnote 28 of the Opinion strongly suggests, in these circumstances, that the lawyer perform research into the identity of the seller.
- You may refuse to aid in the purchase, although you are not expected, or permitted, to report the client to law enforcement.

Unsatisfactory answers from the client means the lawyer should think twice about entering into the ACR.

*Scenario No. 3*: The Case of the Lawyer Who Went Bad Very Slowly, then Very Quickly

> Lupe works for a government agency. An agency rule prohibits her from receiving any gift valued at more than $25.00 from lobbyists with whom the agency conducts business or may conduct business. One day she allows a lobbyist—who might do business with the agency—to pay for a gourmet hamburger lunch costing $45.00. Lupe does not self-report the violation, reasoning that the amount was not much more than the dollar limit. The following week she accepts two tickets

(in the bleachers) to a professional baseball game valued at a cost of $100. This pattern continues until she accepts a golf trip to Scotland which she and the lobbyist split 50%/50%; $2,500 each. She rationalizes her conduct by reasoning that since she is paying for part of the trip, she is still an ethical lawyer. This is discovered by the boss who terminates her. She is later indicted and convicted of public corruption.

To understand Lupe, check out the book *Mistakes Were Made (But Not by Me): Why We Justify Foolish Beliefs, Bad Decisions, and Hurtful Acts* by Carol Tavris and Elliot Aronson. What trap did Lupe fall into? According to the authors, she was trapped by cognitive dissonance. The mind cannot hold two competing ideas at the same time—"I am an ethical lawyer" *versus* "I am violating an ethical rule." They point to research that the mind resolves these types of conflict by committing yet *another* ethical violation to justify the preceding violation. The solution: say an emphatic "no" to the first temptation. If you give in to that temptation, then acknowledge to yourself that you violated the rule, self-report, and go forth and sin no more.

### *The Spotlight*

This incremental descent into unethical conduct caused the Watergate scandal in 1973, leading to disbarment, prison time, and the resignation of then-President Richard Nixon. Mark Curriden, "The Lawyers of Watergate: How a '3rd-Rate Burglary' Provoked New Standards for Lawyer Ethics." *ABA Journal* published June 1, 2012. To recap: low level Republican operatives were caught burglarizing the headquarters of the Democratic party in the Watergate complex in Washington, D.C. Lawyers, including White House counsel John Dean, tried to cover up the involvement of higher-ups. They failed, ultimately involving President Nixon, a lawyer himself. (By the way, it was this lawyer's involvement that caused the ABA to mandate the Professional Responsibility course you took.) Former Assistant U.S. Attorney Eric Overby from Ohio wrote a perspective letter to the ABA Journal about the article which perfectly sums up going bad. Here it is:

Mr. Dean spoke at my law school circa 1979 and made an indelible impression. To paraphrase, he said that he (and others) didn't wake up one day and say, "Let's go break the law." He said every day, every decision was one step closer to "the line." Each step was small, but one day he turned around and realized he had crossed the line a long time ago and didn't even know it. I've incorporated what Dean said into ethics discussions I've led by saying, "There are no points awarded for how close you can get to the cliff before you fall over. If you see the cliff, move away from it—not closer to it."

*Lesson: To paraphrase Oscar Wilde: "We can resist anything except temptation." So stay away from situations that can lead to ethical trouble.*

## Tool No. 3: Communicate the ACR Terms

While putting every engagement agreement in writing is good advice, it's only partial advice. What really matters are the terms that are put in writing, not merely that it's in writing. As we see in the following Tell and Show, there is an art to this type of communication.

### Tell and Show

You have met with the client and discussed the client's objectives. (Recall from Model Rule 1.2 that the client sets the objectives, and the lawyer "abides" by the client's decisions.)

Every ACR should start with an engagement communication (usually a letter) which is simply a written document setting out what you will do, but just as importantly, what you will not do. A lack of clarity in these terms can lead to grievances filed and malpractice lawsuits brought.

***By Way of Illustration:***

- Limited Engagement Agreement

In the following limited engagement agreement, notice how the lawyer specifically communicates the lawyer's obligations with restrictive language:

> This engagement is **limited** to representation of client **in connection** with the negotiation of a settlement with Company. As a result, I will **<u>not</u>** represent Client **in any other matter**, including the filing of a lawsuit, unless a new representation agreement is signed by the parties with respect to such new matter, which may include new and different terms.

Let's give another example in a non-litigation context, with a slightly different communication emphasis:

A client is considering investing in a business and retains you to determine whether the business is properly registered to conduct business in your state. To effectively communicate with the Client, consider listing in the engagement communication what you will not do and (here's the slightly different emphasis) also list what you will not do but that a client *could* perhaps assume you will do such as:

- Determining the viability of its business model;
- Providing an opinion on the credit worthiness of the company; or
- Issuing an opinion on whether the investment is wise.

When the investment goes sour, who does the client sue for malpractice? That's right, the law firm it retained and hired. *See* Smookler v. Kronish Lieb Weiner & Hellman, LLP, 2006 N.Y.Misc. LEXIS 3982 (N.Y. Sup. Ct., Jan. 11, 2006) (Summary Judgment granted to the law firm based on the specified services that were explicitly ***<u>not</u>*** included in the engagement communication).

➢ Gain Client Commitment to Your Ethical Obligations

Get a Pre-Commitment in the engagement communication. Consider terms like these:

> Client understands that Lawyer has ethical obligations contained in the Model Rules which Lawyer has discussed with client. Client agrees that if she insists that Lawyer violate one or more of these rules, that Lawyer will have the option to withdraw from

representation and Client agrees to assist with such withdrawal.

Here, the Pre-Commitment confirms the client's agreement that the lawyer must abide by certain ethical standards. We know of the obligations; most clients do not. A Pre-Commitment avoids springing them on the client after the ACR is well underway. Here is how it works: At the start of an ACR we all suffer from "projection bias" which is nothing more than the belief that how we will feel in the future is exactly how we feel right now. And the start of an ACR is all good vibes. The power of this bias is compounded by the commitment bias. Cognitive researcher Dan Pilat writes: "[This bias] stipulates that we tend to remain committed to our past behaviors regardless of how we feel in the moment, deciding to pre-commit to a particular behavior is likely to keep us bound to our resolutions even when our motivation wanes."

*Lesson: As playwright George Bernard Shaw reflected, the challenge with communication is the illusion that it occurred. The engagement communication provides the lawyer with an opportunity to communicate in transparent and clear terms to the Client. Take it.*

## Tool No. 4: Communicate About Fees

A challenge faced by many lawyers, especially new ones, is discussing with a client how much to charge for their legal services. Let's face it: most of us are uncomfortable discussing money in general and are doubly uncomfortable discussing how much money a client pays to us for our legal work.

But when you do, remind yourself that you went to college, took the LSAT, attended law school for three or more years, studied for and passed the bar exam. You spent a lot of time learning and preparing to be a lawyer. So, value yourself and the time and money you invested in becoming a lawyer. That is why the client has come to you.

### Tell and Show

Many new lawyers believe irrationally that they are unworthy of charging a fee. They feel guilty when they see a bill that will be sent to a person they often know and like and may even consider as a friend.

The lawyer fears the client will no longer like them if a bill is sent, "I thought we were friends!" But it is not about the lawyer, it's about the client's need to "trust" their lawyer, and, much trust is gained through one tool of communication, namely, transparency. Model Rule 1.5(b) sets the communication baseline:

> "(The) basis or rate of the fee and expenses for which the client will be responsible shall be communicated to the client, preferably in writing, before or within a reasonable time after commencing the representation. . ."

***By Way of Illustration:***

Trust is further enhanced with the following communication tools demonstrating transparency:

- **First Meeting.** During the first meeting provide a comprehensive overview of the services to be provided and fees/costs tethered to them. Be clear on the identity of the lawyers who will be working on the matter and their respective roles. Transparency is frustrated and trust impaired if the client concludes—even if erroneously—that a bait and switch is going on.
- **On Invoices.** What You Did vs. What You Provided. Stating only what you did leaves the client wondering about what was done and why. Effective communication answers possible client questions in advance. If a lawyer only includes the former, then the lawyer is missing a prime opportunity to communicate their value and to educate the client. What looks better to the client: "Appeared at preliminary Temporary Injunction hearing" or "Represented client at Temporary Injunction hearing to argue for dismissal of unfounded claim." The difference is between passivity and action, between relaying information to the client and developing a bond with the client.

- **What You *Won't* Bill For.** From time to time write "No charge." For instance, at the conclusion of the representation, and without charging the client, prepare a short "After Action Report" (a tradition in the military) detailing what went well and how the client can do more of that, and what did not go so well (and how a client can fix the shortcomings). This is not done to assign blame or to parse out praise, but rather to leave the client better off than when the representation started. There is no better way to communicate "thanks for your business."

*Lesson: Embrace transparency.*

### FINDING YOUR VOICE

- Research the average hourly fee of a lawyer practicing in the area of law that you do practice or hope to practice. Consider your first few clients in this area of law. Draft an explanation of why the hourly rate is reasonable, and what is likely to be achieved for the expected total cost. What are some alternate outcomes for the matter, and how will you address them with the client up front? How can you reasonably keep the client informed of fees and expenses, as or before they occur?
- Consider a client or type of client you would like to have. Do the research to learn more about their industry, their particular business, their anticipated legal needs, as the case may be. What questions would you ask to learn more about their needs and objectives? How might you demonstrate your openness to learning, and not just tell them what you can do?

## Tool No. 5: Create an ACR Formation Task List

There is a lot to keep track of when communicating with a new client during the process of ACR formation. Our advice is to consider using an ACR Formation Checklist. You can update over time, tailoring it to your personal preferences and the needs of your practice.

## Tell and Show

The following was inspired by Patrick A. Talley Jr., the 2024–2025 President of the Louisiana Bar Association. President Talley is on point: "Communication is key to a positive attorney-client relationship. Ideally, communication with the client should not be set out as a discrete task; it should be part of every action you take (as a lawyer). However, so many attorneys have difficulty with this aspect of representation. . ."

We created the following two checklists to help in meeting this Challenge:

*Checklist No. 1: ACR Formation*

☑ Does the client understand the scope of the representation?

☑ Does the client understand the type of fee arrangement, what fees or costs are charged, why, and when they apply?

☑ Does the client understand how client trust money will be used?

☑ Have you developed all the facts to make sure that the client's objectives have a good faith basis?

☑ Does the client understand what additional, if any, further actions are required on their part?

☑ Do you understand exactly what it is that the client wants you to do?

The checklist above sets out the core inquiries. The subsections below correspond to those same items and outline potential communication points you may need to address with the client.

*Checklist No. 2: Opportunities for Communication*

**☑ Does the client understand the scope of the representation?**

*Opportunity to communicate, if applicable:*

- Limited scope of proffered services.
- Representation not provided.

- Who at the firm will be providing legal services.

☑ **Does the client understand the type of fee arrangement, what fees or costs are charged, why, and what they will apply to?**

*Opportunity to communicate, if applicable:*

- Fixed fee, contingency fee, hourly fee
- The costs you bear and the costs that the client may need to pay directly or reimburse you for such as copying, expert witness fees, computerized legal research, deposition transcription, and expenses.

☑ **Does the client understand how client trust money will be used?**

*Opportunity to communicate, if applicable:*

- The purpose of the trust account and the mechanics of how money is transferred from it to your operating account.
- Whether trust funds will be applied to monthly invoices, and when and how the trust fund will be replenished.
- That funds not used in the trust account will be returned to the client.
- The concept of IOLTA and who sets and receives the interest on client money in the account.

☑ **Have you developed all the facts to make sure that the client's objectives have a good faith basis?**

*Opportunity to communicate, if applicable:*

- That you are ethically bound by ABA Model Rule 3.1: Meritorious Claims and Contentions, to assert claims that have a good faith basis (that is, one with a concrete factual basis not a conjectural one), although you will be developing more facts during the discovery phase of any litigation.

☑ **Does the client understand what additional, if any, further actions are required on their part?**

*Opportunity to communicate, if applicable:*

- Additional documents that the client must provide to you.
- The need for the client's timeline of events.
- Whether there should be an attempt at settlement before litigation commences.
- The need to preserve all data and information, including on phones, tablets, computers, and the like.

☑ **Do you understand *exactly* what it is that the client wants you to do?**

- Ask the client what they want, as well as offering potential legal options.
- Repeat the agreed objective(s) out loud. This is the legal version of 10-4 which, according to the Urban Dictionary, means "Okay; Understood; and Affirmative".

And how do you determine whether the client understands? Do not accept a simple "I get it" from the client. Rather, ask open ended questions such as:

➢ "What questions do you have?" (This is good because it *presumes* there is a question.)

➢ "What are your thoughts?" (Another presumption.)

➢ "What do you not fully understand?"

➢ "What could I explain more fully to ensure that I am doing a good job in communicating these terms?"

➢ "I know this is a lot to take in. Now is a good time to ask questions. What are they?" (This communication technique normalizes ignorance as an acceptable. Clients will not ask from a fear of looking dumb. Do not allow your clients to be held hostage to this fear.)

*Lesson: It is our job to ensure understanding, not the client's.*

## Tool No. 6: The Power of Humility

*Humility* and *Power*. Two words not often associated, but they should be. Why do we in the legal profession think we have to be know-it-alls? Maybe because people who are not lawyers treat us like we can solve all of their legal quandaries, from traffic tickets to an old criminal record from college. Even when our practice area is commercial real estate or business litigation. This starts in law school, doesn't it? And it never ends. Or maybe it's because we must walk into so many arenas with confidence, on behalf of our clients. The expectations, and the environment, can make us feel that we really should be the last word, the Jack (or Jill or Jae) of all trades, the only adult in the room.

### Tell and Show

Throughout your career you will be invited to pitch to a potential new client, answer client questions in the middle of representation, address matters that have not yet been brought to you for formal representation, and lead activities from depositions to court hearings to trials where all eyes are on you. Bet you think you must walk in as the omniscient and all-powerful Lawyer with a capital "L." Not so.

***By Way of Illustration:***

In truth, nobody likes a know-it-all. And behaving as if we know all the answers when in fact we do not only leads to error. Take for example the attorney taking the deposition of an expert witness. When the expert references a term or phrase or conclusion not entirely familiar to the counsel opposite, what is the best response? One response is to act is if you already know all about that. . .thing. Another response, better calculated to lead to full and complete information for you and your client, is to ask questions: What do you mean by that? Will you explain that answer? Can you break that down for me? That face of bravado in the teeth of unclear information is useful to nobody—least of all, the client. Never leave the deposition without understanding exactly what was said, and what is behind it. Doing otherwise is a waste of your time and the client's money.

***By Way of Illustration:***

Or take the lawyer who shows up to pitch a client, and rambles on about themselves, their experience, their law firm, plus how they might resolve the problems the lawyer anticipates for this business or person, which may not be the problems they actually experience at all. The client will probably feel the way you might feel if a banker who wants your business shows up and talks about the golf tournaments their bank sponsors and the lines of credit they offer when, in fact, you have no interest in either. How much better is it to ask questions about the client, their business, their long-term and immediate needs and goals, their experience with legal representation. Now, that's humility. You can still show your experience (what we may call "credentialing") by good and pointed questions (e.g., Do you have a company agreement? What is your corporate structure? What is the tiebreaker if you and your partners are at an impasse? What is the role of your board?). But only ask such questions when the client is done telling you about themselves and what is on their mind.

***By Way of Illustration:***

Humility means acknowledging that you need time to brief a new topic raised in the middle of a hearing, instead of blustering your way through. Judges can smell a bluster a mile away. It means acknowledging that you don't understand the legal or factual basis for a claim made by the other side, and asking for clarification, instead of assuming they don't know what they are talking about. It means asking your expert to help you prepare for the deposition of an opposing expert, instead of believing you can learn everything there is to know about someone else's career specialty from articles on the internet. It means asking to meet your clients at their place of business so you can see their operations and better understand what they do. It means asking the legal team—including those without law degrees—for a gut check on your decision making.

At every turn, humility means a stance of openness and curiosity. The natural outcome is a deeper, richer understanding of the matters you are handling. Posturing has its limited place, such as mediation. But the reality is that humility is power. It is powerful because it leads to better information and thus a better ability to represent and advise your client. Information and understanding give you an edge that bravado never will.

*Lesson: Read Jim Murphy's book, Inner Excellence: Train Your Mind for Extraordinary Performance and the Best Possible Life. One message: being humble is being strong. His example: the Navy Seals who never forget that the enemy has a vote.*

## The Challenge: How Do I Start a Client Interview?

AI tools will never replace the lawyer's role in interviewing a client. Interviewing involves much more than merely a Q & A session with a client. All legal matters—litigation or transactional—involve the surface facts *and* a story beneath the surface. There are multiple dynamics at play.

## Tool No. 1: Get Foundational Information

It is understandable that you want to get to the facts and prove your worth. But plan for future communication issues. Here is a checklist on what to ask for before jumping in:

### Tell and Show

- ☑ All contact information—all names ever used, all addresses used, all phone numbers used
- ☑ Emergency contact information
- ☑ Immigration status
- ☑ Preference for how best to communicate
- ☑ Best times to call
- ☑ Information that will be asked in discovery—driver's license, work documents etc.
- ☑ Social media accounts (often asked for in discovery especially in personal injury lawsuits)

*Lesson: Before getting to the facts, start with the basics.*

### Tool No. 2: Have a Friendly Talk About the Client's Social Media

This might be a hard conversation. Clients view their private life as private, balking at the idea that their social media could somehow be relevant to their lawsuit.

### Tell and Show

- *Ineffective Communication:*

  Lawyer: Client, make sure you do not delete anything from your social media.

  Client: Sure.

  Was the message received? Maybe yes, maybe no.

- *Effective Communication:*

  Lawyer: My experience in these types of cases is that the other side will ask us to give them all of your social media (list examples). While I know this might seem like an intrusion into your life, it is fair game. You are claiming an injury, and they would want to see if you commented on it or posted photos of yourself. So, make sure you do not delete any social media. After all, we do not want to be in the position of telling the judge that you did and then having to stand in front of her and explain why. I know this is a lot of info to take in. If you have any questions, now is the time to ask.

  Client: Well, I do have this question. . .

*Lesson: Remember there is an ethical duty to preserve evidence or potential evidence under MR 3.4 (a): Fairness to Opposing Party and Counsel. And this duty entails communicating clearly to your client regarding their (and your) duties.*

## Tool No. 3: Explain the Attorney-Client Privilege

Client attention will be high at the start. So, this message will be more readily and easily absorbed. And starting here negates a client fear, often unspoken, about the confidentiality of what is told to you. We use "explain" very deliberately. A dictionary tells us "Explain" means "to name an idea clearly to someone by describing it in more detail or by revealing relevant facts or ideas."

### Tell and Show

Why go into more detail than simply saying "Our conversations are protected by the attorney-client privilege?"

First, because of clients. Clients are often hesitant to tell us the entire truth. Always recall that the practice of law is as much about understanding human nature as it is about understanding substantive legal principles. And human nature teaches us that clients hold back because it is only natural to feel embarrassed when you mess up or believe you messed up. And we do not want others—yes, even our lawyers—to know that we zigged when we should have zagged. (We will talk more about this in the Tool on Being Non-Judgmental.) So, try something along these lines:

> *Lawyer:* Let's talk about the attorney-client privilege. Have you heard of it?
>
> *Client:* Yeah. I hear about it in movies and TV shows like Suits.
>
> *Lawyer:* What do you understand that it means?
>
> *Client:* That all this is private?
>
> *Lawyer:* Pretty much. When you come to me for legal advice then what you say and how I advise you is just between you and me. The person you want to sue cannot find out about anything we talk about, from me or from you. The reason we have this rule is so that you feel free to tell me everything.
>
> *Client:* Sounds good.

*Lawyer:* A few things to keep in mind. If you tell anyone else about what we say, then the privilege no longer applies. In fact, a question the lawyer working for the person you sue might ask when he takes your sworn testimony before trial is, "Have you spoken to anyone about what you and your lawyer talked about?" And if you say "yes" then the lawyer can ask you what was said and we lose the confidentiality about all of our strategies to win your case, or how much money we would accept to settle the case, for example. We spend a lot of time in law school learning about the attorney client privilege so it's only natural if you might have a question or thought now or later about it. Do you?

Second, because of lawyers. Yes us! Ever hear of the "curse of knowledge"? Law professors can be infected with it as well as practicing lawyers. Once you understand something, we tend to make assumptions that *everyone* understands. It is hard to remember there was a time when we did not know it.

*Lesson: Be direct. Be empathetic. Be strategic.*

## Tool No. 4: Prepare Your Mindset for the Interview

Now you can get to the factual substance of the client's concerns.

### Tell and Show

A few tips about this discussion that are necessary to note:

➤ **Do Not Follow a Script or List of Questions**

It is fine to set an agenda for the interview. "We will talk first about ABC and then EFG." This allows you to divide the interview into chunks and then transition from one chunk to next, "Such as 'now that we have gone over ABC, let's move on to EFG.' "

But it is not fine to rigidly adhere to a set script or list of questions. We know that the thought of going without a detailed script/outline might seem like performing a high wire act without the benefit of a safety net underneath, especially when it comes to interpersonal interactions. But client interviewing is an organic process, not a scripted one. It's not a play. You've spent the last three years practicing how to interview a client; after all, the Socratic method is nothing more than question and answer becoming the foundation for a follow up question and the next answer, and so on.

So, prepare a set of foundation questions as a framework, *not* as a formula. When a client answers a particular question allow yourself a few minutes to think and process the answer. The next logical question will come to you.

➢ **Do Not Internalize**

Some clients will be angry or disappointed. Clients may see you as part of a system that does not represent them or their best interests. By way of example, a court-appointed lawyer may deal with clients seeing them as part of a corrupt system that is prosecuting them in the first place. Internalizing makes the interaction about you, not the client. Take a breath. Let the client vent.

➢ **Do Not Multi-Task**

Prepare to focus on the client. Your actions communicate as well as your words. If you appear to be giving less than 100% attention to the client, then the client will mirror what she sees, giving half-hearted attention to questions or comments. If there is a true emergency brewing, then be transparent with the client, "I know we have set aside this time to go over your matter, but there is a possible emergency with another client, and I may have to interrupt our meeting." Finally, with your tablet or smart phone, turn off notifications and put it in your briefcase or bag, out of sight.

*Lesson: Effective interviewing is more than just getting the four W's—Who, What, When, Why.*

**The Neurodiversity Insight**

Do Not Internalize. But if you are neurodivergent, this is easier said than done, especially if you struggle with the executive function skills of emotional regulation. Emotional regulation is when you internally go from one extreme to another and it takes a lot of effort to bring yourself back to neutral. Failure to re-regulate leads to internal overthinking, ruminating and anxiety. There is no quick fix for this, although you've probably heard at least some strategies for re-regulating emotions:

Physical needs: get enough sleep regularly, eat a healthy diet, and exercise. Simple yet hard to do regularly.

Sense of Achievement: even if you love your job, you'll have a few bad days. Instead of ruminating on the bad, identify one positive thing in that day. It doesn't have to be work related or a "big" thing, but maybe something as simple as "I got up on time." Consider creating a "One Good Thing" log where you keep a running list of one good thing every day. This can be a Word doc or a written list, and the value in keeping the log is that it creates the habit, and you are reminded of a lot of "one good things."

Thoughts vs. Feelings: change your thoughts instead of your feelings. When you feel dis-regulated ask yourself what you are thinking that is causing you to feel a certain way? Why are you reacting so strongly, what is the worst that could happen, how important will this be tomorrow? Next month? Next year?

## Tool No. 5: Discover the Story Beneath the Surface

Clients rarely come to a lawyer with a plan to deceive the lawyer. But they will come with all too human traits: fearing looking dumb, seeing matters emotionally, vaguely considered goals and objectives. It is your job to penetrate the noise and get to the signal.

## Tell and Show

### ➢ Do Ask About What You Sense Is Going on

Many of you are naturally empathetic individuals. This is a positive. Too often lawyers discount the value of their intuition. The topic is seldom mentioned in law school but is valuable for lawyers. We define it as rapid cognition and foresight. A safe way to test whether you are right is simply to say, "I get the sense that you are worried about XYZ. . ." and then trail off and listen to the response. Saying it this way works, as opposed to the declarative, "I see you are worried about XYZ. . ." Other methods to gauge the true story beneath the surface:

- Can you provide more details about what brought you here to seek legal help?
- What concerns or worries you most about this matter?
- How has this situation affected you personally? Practically?

### ➢ Do Ask Open Ended Questions

These types of questions cast a wide net in developing a broad base of information. You can then drill down from there. Illustrations are, "Can you tell me more about that?" or "Can you go into greater detail than that?" They work especially well if you are unsure of where to take the interview or are unsure of what the client is feeling or thinking.

### ➢ Do Be Sensitive About Sensitive Topics

Use "door openers" through which you essentially ask permission to get into the sensitive topics included in most any representation. An example for drafting a will, "Can we talk now about who is identified as a beneficiary in your will?" (and by implication you are inviting them to tell you who is being left out if they want to go there) or in a business dispute over the ownership of a business, "Would you like to tell me about the early days of starting your business with Mr. Smith?" or "Can you tell me what you might see as being an ideal conclusion to this matter?" Note that these questions invite not merely a factual recitation but invite a discussion on the emotional dimensions of the matter as well.

*Lesson: As with effective physicians, do not merely treat the symptoms of the condition, but treat the underlying cause of the condition.*

## Tool No. 6: Be Nonjudgmental

Judgmental means arriving at a conclusion before fully developing the facts. In the initial substantive interview, a lawyer must rise above the inclination to be judgmental. This means more than just moral judgments.

Sometimes when we are judgmental and act like non-lawyers, we hear a few facts, jump to a conclusion, and gap-fill what comes next. Preemptive judgment clouds the efficacy of our fact-gathering and, therefore, taints the usefulness of our ultimate legal advice.

### Tell and Show

Being judgmental is all too human, argues Andrew McMasters in his book, *Listening Without Agenda: Practical Steps for Effective Listening.* Citing psychologist Daniel Kahneman, McMasters notes that there are two types of thinking: Type 1 which is fast and unconscious, and Type 2 which is slower and more deliberate. For developing pertinent facts, lawyers should use Type 2 thinking.

When we use Type 1 thinking we often arrive at false conclusions. For example, consider when a colleague is late to a meeting. Our minds create a belief that the person is disorganized and rude, when there might be other circumstances—which you know nothing about—causing the tardy entrance.

McMasters writes that, "[t]raining our brain to slow down and let go of inner judgment is the hard work we have to engage in to be an effective listener." How do we train our brain to accomplish this goal? What should we do and not do to create a judgment-free zone, to find out what happened?

***By Way of Illustration:***

**What *Not* to Do**

➢ *Do not ask close-ended questions*

They have their place, but not when developing the pertinent facts. A close-ended question is often phrased as a multiple choice, true/false or yes/no. Lawyer who ask these types of questions appear to the client to have already reached a judgment about the matter.

Example: "Were you angry about getting fired from work?" can be answered in one word, stifling further factual development.

➢ *Do not interrupt*

Let clients finish their thoughts before responding or asking a clarifying question. Yes, at some point you may need to control the interview, but understand that how clients set out their narratives, the words they use, and the order in which they use them is often useful information.

➢ *Do not try to mind read*

Do not assume you know what they will say (talk about jumping to conclusions). Even if you have heard similar facts, this is your client's individual experience, and they need to feel heard, seen, and understood. If you find yourself filling in the client's sentences, or completing their thoughts, then hit Full Stop!

**What to Do**

➢ *Adhere to Unconditional Positive Regard*

Psychotherapist Carl Rogers coined this term which is the essence of a state of non-judgment. It consists of:

- Accepting clients for who they are, regardless of their behavior or beliefs. "I am not here to judge you. I am here to help you with your legal issues" or "We all fall short at some time; the question is how we respond to it and that is 100% within our control."

- Treat all clients with respect and dignity even when you disagree with their actions or decisions. "Hindsight is 20/20. We all, at one time or another, zigged when we should have zagged."

*Lesson: Be understanding. Be accepting. Be open-minded.*

**The Neurodiversity Insight No. 1**

Assess the accessibility of your environment. This is relevant because the environment can either help or hinder communication between the lawyer and client. Being inclusive benefits everyone, not just those who are neurodivergent. You would not think twice about using closed captioning for a client who is hard of hearing or closing the blinds to prevent the sun from shining directly in someone's eyes. A neurodivergent client is a client, and you want to make sure they can fully engage.

When it comes to interactions, two of the most common differences between neurotypical and neurodivergent are small-talk and eye contact.

Small Talk: Recognize that small talk is different for neurodivergent individuals. Neurodivergent people understand that conversations are important interactions to build connection. But from the neurodiverse perspective, neurotypicals talk to each other about things for no reason. The surface level of conversation is what a neurodivergent person sees as a waste of time and wants to disengage. A neurodivergent person wants to have a conversation, and it should be meaningful. They want to see if they have compatible views so why do we need to waste all this time with "chit chat?"

> Neurotypical person: the chit chat gets the conversation going and it's how you build connections.
>
> Neurodivergent person: that is not how you build connections, build them by talking about things we're interested in and sharing experiences and to do this,

we must constantly self-monitor and keep an inner dialogue going.

Eye Contact: Neurotypicals think eye contact is important. For many neurodivergent people, this is not something they can do without consciously making themselves do it. When they are in a conversation where they have to make eye contact, they are on high alert and expending a lot of energy telling themselves to look at the person and make the "right" eye contact and also asking themselves if they are doing it right, and they hope they're not being weird, but they have no way to tell.

**The Neurodiversity Insight No. 2**

When a neurotypical person is talking about something that happened to them, a neurodivergent person might share a similar experience to show we are listening, and we understand. It is how we relate to what you are saying. Apparently, that is often not how neurotypical people perceive it—to them, it appears self-centered. In an ideal world, everyone would know that this is how some neurodivergent individuals show empathy, but the reality is that many individuals, including clients, do not know this. As attorneys, it is our responsibility to make sure our clients do not confuse empathy with self-centeredness.

## Tool No. 7: Listen!

In achieving a client-focused interview, and remaining nonjudgmental, Rogers emphasized the importance of active listening—what we call engaged listening. Through engaged listening a client feels heard, understood, and validated. These feelings encourage a greater client willingness to open up about all facts—good and bad, flattering and damning.

### Tell and Show

Business professors Jeffrey Yip and Colin M. Fisher extensively researched effective listening, publishing their conclusions in, "Are You Really a Good Listener?" in the May-June 2025 edition of the *Harvard Business Review*. Because lawyers have much to learn from sister professions, we use their article as a framework for lawyers.

➤ **Do Not Listen in Haste**

"[L]istening in haste can be worse than not listening at all." True in business, true in conducting client interviews. You encourage others to be more thorough and transparent with you when you show you truly care about what they are saying. So, they do not feel rushed, set aside dedicated time for an interview.

Doing so sends the signal to the client that you are invested in hearing what the client says, and nothing important will be missed or glossed over.

➤ **Do Not Be Defensive**

We advise that you PPI, Presume Positive Intent on their part, which means that you recognize you are both on the same side and have the same goals. If you need time to return to a PPI mindset, buy time by simply restating what you think the client is saying and sincerely thank them for sharing. This buying of time also prevents the lawyer from lashing back at the client.

➤ **Do Manage Anger**

Anger is a more difficult matter to handle, but it can be done. First, you need to remember that the case is not only about "the case." It is also about something much more, especially in family, probate, and employment law. The psychologist Dr. Abraham Maslow described a person's hierarchy of needs. Clients have them too. They need to be acknowledged, emotionally heard, and respected. Visualize the hierarchy as a triangle with these needs at the apex. Starting and ending with the technical solutions, which forms the triangle's base, without considering the apex needs, can be disastrous.

For instance, let's look at a meeting that Professor Maslanka had with a CEO of a new client. At the outset he said, "[a]ll lawyers are leeches, interested only in padding their pockets, and you guys are not much better than the suing employee trying to take me down." His reaction? Rather than getting defensive or arguing with him, he acknowledged his feelings. Once he knew he was heard, and empathized with, he was able to get the meeting back on track.

➢ **Do Be Present**

As stressed earlier, be present. Let's elaborate on this idea. It is essential that you provide visible signs of engagement. You must communicate to the client that you are present for them. Use phrases to demonstrate this, as with, "Is it fine with you if I take some notes as we talk?" or using simple phrases such as "I see" or "That makes sense." These phrases signal that you are following along, honoring their perspectives, and trying to process their responses to you. Or you can use body language—what researchers call "back channeling."

Consider nodding or looking up at the client from your notes or adopting an open posture in your seat while talking to the client. And as we mentioned earlier, summarizing. The authors of the article describe summarizing as a "powerful" way to confirm your understanding of another. "So, what I'm hearing is that you are concerned about your estranged son challenging your will" is an example. This technique reassures the client that you are indeed listening and prevents misunderstandings.

➢ **Do Avoid Exhaustion**

"Exhaustion is a silent killer of effective listening," warns the authors. We agree. Being dedicated to the law does not mean that you are impervious to the wear and tear, the rough and tumble of our profession. Schedule interviews when you are fresh. Doing so communicates that you care.

➢ **Do Take Some Action After Interviewing**

A failure to follow up after the interview erodes the trust you have built up with the client. Do something, even if it is only an email saying thanks and setting out a timeline of what is coming next. Try and refer to the substance of the interview, summarize the agreed upon goals from the interview or confirm a To Do List. *Show* the client you listened.

*Lesson: Don't say you care, show you care.*

**The Neurodiversity Insight**

Listening takes a lot of energy. Because it is easy to get exhausted with an interview, neurodivergent lawyers should not ignore the coming challenge and should adjust your processes to accommodate your needs. One suggestion is clearing the clutter. Before you start an interview, clean off your desk (or at least move your piles elsewhere). This will make focusing on the client easier. Limit yourself to just your immediate workspace (your desk) so you do not get distracted or fixated on clearing ALL the clutter or feel overwhelmed by the size of the task. Use a box of time (11:00am–11:30 am) or use the Two Minute Rule (work on this for two minutes and stop.) Set your smartphone alarm for the boxed time.

## Tool No. 8: Corralling the Ramble

There will be times, however, when a lawyer needs to consider asserting control over a client interview. Clients can ramble and you need to refocus them. Depending on the circumstances, try one of the following:

### Tell and Show

(1) "Let's come back to that point later, but first. . ."

(2) "I want to make sure I understand this better, so could you share. . ."

(3) "It sounds as if this is important, but before we delve into it, I want to focus on our current topic. . ."

(4) "I promise that we will get into everything you think is important, but this will go more efficiently if we focus for now on. . .

(5) "On one hand you say ABC is the case, yet on the other you claim XYZ. Can you clear this up for me?"

***By Way of Illustration:***

A useful gesture when a client ramble comes to us from the sports world. It is the "T" gesture where one hand is held horizontally and the other vertically. This is universally understood to mean "time out." It is a variation of what we talked about earlier about using your hands.

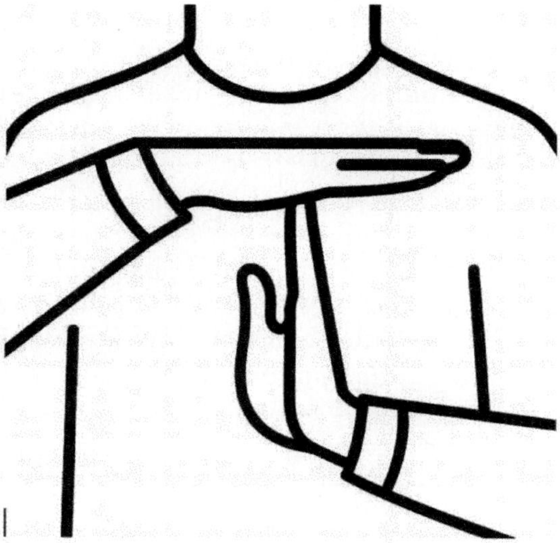

*Lesson: While clients are responsible for the content of an interview, we are responsible for its structure.*

## The Challenge: How Do I Develop a Counseling Style?

The dynamics of client counseling are at the heart of the attorney-client relationship. There are different styles, their use often depends on the needs of the client and the issue at hand. Moreover, there are specific tools you can adopt as you see fit for the moment. This will add up, over time, to finding *your* style.

## Tool No. 1: Think About a Counseling Mindset

There are different models of counseling. Dr. Atul Gawande in "*Being Mortal: Medicine and What Matters in the End*" describes several models used by doctors based on the work of two medical ethicists, Drs. Ezekiel and Linda Emanuel from our sister profession. With some editorial changes, here they are:

➢ **The Authority Approach**

"I went to medical school, and I'm trained and therefore I am telling you to take the red pill, not the blue one, because it will be good for you." Dr. Gawande sums this up as an approach in which the doctor tells the patient what she needs to know. As he tells it, this is a common approach, which he describes as a "priestly, doctor knows best model. . .(used) especially with vulnerable patients—the frail, the poor, the elderly, and anyone who tends to do what they're told."

➢ **The Informative Approach**

He writes that this mindset is the opposite of the authority approach. He sums it up: "The doctor is the technical expert. The patient is the consumer." In other words, the doctor says to the patient, "here's what the red pill does, and here is what the blue pill does" and you decide which one you want. This works well when the choices are clear, the trade-offs are easily understood, and people may simply prefer one treatment over the other.

➢ **The Interpretive Approach**

Here, doctors query patients on their goals; their priorities; their worries. Then and only then does the doctor explain what the red and blue bills do and the one that will help achieve their priorities. This is known in medical circles as shared decision-making.

Each has its place depending on the client's situation and on the client's needs.

*Lesson: Notice how the approaches go from the most direct to the most nuanced. Think about using the one that fits your situation.*

## Tool No. 2: Use the Ethical Rules

When it comes to developing your counseling style, Tool No. 1 intersects with the Model Rules and the counseling values they embrace.

### Tell and Show

By way of example, MR 2.1 is labeled as the "Advisor" rule and permits a lawyer to treat clients holistically. Here is its language:

"In rendering advice, a lawyer may refer not only to law but to other considerations such as moral, economic, social and political factors, which may be relevant to the client's situation."

This obligation is why we get to call ourselves not only "Attorneys" but "Attorneys and Counselors-at-Law."

***By Way of Illustration:***

A landlord client is planning on evicting an 87-year-old widow for being two months behind on her rent. The landlord instructs you to begin the eviction process. You can counsel that doing so is a bad look from a public relations standpoint and offer options to the client such as spreading the past due rent payment over time or offering assistance to move to a less expensive apartment. But you cannot make the decision for the client. We will look at how to help clients expand their options in later tools in this section.

***By Way of Illustration:***

MR 2.1 dovetails with MR 1.2: Scope of Representation and Allocation of Authority Between Client and Lawyer, which mandates that a lawyer:

"(s)hall abide by a client's decisions concerning the objectives of representation . . . (and) shall consult with the client as to the means by which they are to be pursued."

Let's deconstruct. Dating from Biblical times, "Abide" means to "stay, remain, or continue in a place or relationship." Applied to lawyering, it conveys the message that, while a lawyer must follow the client's lawful objectives, a lawyer can nevertheless still seek to change the client's mind about those objectives.

The client is on death row awaiting execution. You find new case law providing a viable argument to reduce the sentence to life imprisonment. The client is competent to make decisions and tells you "Forget these new arguments. I deserve to die. Time to meet my maker." And so, you must refrain from making further appeals on his behalf, while still advocating for him to change his mind. *Red Dog v. State*, 625 A.2d 245 (Del. 1993).

*Lesson: Think holistically.*

## Tool No. 3: Reframe Negatives into Positives

Law school trains lawyers in the art of the negative. Consider the issue-spotting exams typical of law school, which are doled out for identifying problems and not always solutions. But clients come to us for the latter, not the former. So, arm yourself with this counseling tool.

### Tell and Show

In his astute book, *The Art of Advice*, Jeswald W. Salacuse, former dean of the Southern Methodist University Dedman School of Law, made a telling point:

> A pessimistic advisor is generally not the best advisor. Indeed, consistently negative advice is often an indication of inexperience. While formal education might have taught advisors what won't work, it's experience that teaches them what will.

Being optimistic is not being a Pollyanna; it is not adopting an ostrich-like attitude of self-delusion; it is not a willful refusal to see the obvious. Rather, the essence of optimism is developing and presenting options which will solve the client's needs. Any lawyer can essentially "C.Y.A." to avoid exposure by *not* doing something. Clients do not need to pay for this—if the answer is wholly binary, black and white, the client does not need us. A flipped quarter does the job as well. Rather, it is up to the lawyer to develop options among shades of gray. In the next Tool we will discuss how to develop options.

For now, we focus on Dean Salacuse's telling point: "One of the talents of effective advisors is to make the clients see the positive opportunities in a situation, to see the glass is half full rather than half empty, to view a problem as a chance for improvement rather than a certainty for disaster."

It is true that every problem is an opportunity. Note that, when written in Chinese characters, the word for "crisis" is composed of two characters. One represents danger and the other represents opportunity.

***By Way of Illustration:***

Here are illustrations of refraining from Professor Maslanka's life in practice.

*Illustration No. 1: The Case of the Government Investigation*

A corporate client was contacted by a federal government agency. It was investigating why one of their employees was denied health benefits after his termination. Turns out that the client had an absolute rule, no exceptions allowed, whereby continuing health benefits were automatically denied whenever an employee was terminated for a specific reason. Professor Maslanka never thought much of the rule because there was no practical benefit, and because it seemed open to legal attack, and expressed reservations to this effect. The government query only confirmed these fears, although the client ultimately dodged the bullet. It would have been natural, and easy, to have criticized the client for not changing the rule. This does not always involve an overtly critical comment; often, a slight change in the tone of voice, or body language, or a facial expression can just as effectively communicate your displeasure at the situation. Instead of being critical of the client, and lecturing on the law, Professor Maslanka made the following points:

- The complaint from the employee may have done you a favor.

- The regulations dealing with this situation are hieroglyphics and thus hard to understand and implement.
- The claim allows us an opportunity to revisit the policy and consider revisions to it, thus avoiding a more serious problem in the future.

*Illustration No. 2: The Case of the CEO Who Was a Poor Witness*

A case hinged on the testimony of the CEO of a client. She was a poor witness. But as lawyers we owe a duty of candor and undivided loyalty to our clients. The dilemma was delivering the news in a positive frame. Here it was: "Many of the qualities that make Rosa such a dynamic CEO could possibly make her come across as opinionated and rigid to a jury. When in fact she is decisive and self-assured." Note: this was based on the truth about Rosa, not some made up version of Rosa. The mission of effectively communicating about Rosa was accomplished, without being insulting about Rosa.

*Illustration No. 3: The Case of the Blamed Messenger*

Our duty of communicating candidly to a client is not a suicide pact. Our overarching goal is delivering the truth and *still* being around to advise the client. Clients too often conflate the one delivering bad news with an ally now turned into an enemy. Sure, unfair to us but as this book stresses we deal with the law *and* with human nature. Effective communication is the key to threading this needle.

Solution: objectify the bad news which distances the messenger from the message. Try something like the following:

- "While we hotly contest it, we know the other side will (insert bad news) . . ."
- "We can reasonably anticipate that the other side will (insert bad news) . . ."
- "If I was on the other side, I would no doubt bring up (insert bad news)."

*Illustration No. 4: The Case of the Doomed Lawsuit*

Here is a truth: Not every case is a winner. Not by a long shot. Here is another truth: Lawyers always have choices in how they deliver that message.

*Inartful Messaging*

- "It looks as if the other side will prevail."
- "A jury is unpredictable and will likely find against us."
- "I never guaranteed that we would win."

*Artful Messaging*

There are various techniques. Here are two positive-negative sentences effectively delivering bad news while prefacing it with a positive.

- "*While* we relish the opportunity to try a hotly contested case (positive), we are also acutely aware of the dangers of a jury trial (negative)."
- "*While* we acknowledge the many arguments in our favor, we must still face some indisputable and troubling facts."

Or focus on the unfavorable law/case posture:

- "When the facts are filtered through this legal prism. . ."
- "We need to acknowledge that the jury in this venue will undoubtedly be composed of the peers of the plaintiff."

Or impart a shared sense of concern:

- "As difficult as it is for me to say and for you to contemplate. . ."
- "The litigation risk with this type of case—and quite frankly our great frustration with these cases—is that a jury can second-guess your motivations . . ."

*Lesson: As a jury consultant once taught Professor Maslanka: "You can't change the facts, but you can change the story."*

## Tool No. 4: Generate Options for the Client

The case method of law school education also cabins us into a binary or zero-sum mindset, with cases resulting in either (a) a win or (b) a loss. Here, exposing clients to more options is the goal so that the end result is optimal.

### Tell and Show

You are considering buying the latest smartphone with several new video features. It is available at a price of $799.00. Which of the following do you decide to do?

(a) Buy the new and deluxe phone

(b) Not buy the new and deluxe phone.

75% of the subjects would have bought the phone and video and 25% would have passed. But change (a) and (b) to:

(a) Buy the new and deluxe phone

(b) Not buy the new and deluxe phone. Keep the $799.00 for other purchases.

This simple and seemingly obvious change moved the metric to 45% *not* buying the phone.

The business world saw this when Quaker Oats was deciding whether to spend $1.8 billion to buy beverage maker Snapple (it did and it turned out to be a disaster). It would have been well advised to reframe the options into

(a) Buy Snapple

(b) Don't buy Snapple. Keep the $ 1.8 billion for other purchases.

Counselors should start by asking two questions:

(1) What are we giving up by making this choice?

(2) What else could we do with the same time and money?

Read more about such reframing in Chip and Dan Heath's book, "Decisive: How to Make Better Choices in Life and Work."

The application of this insight into legal counseling is profound. Let's say a client is considering filing a lawsuit to protect intellectual property from infringement. How much will the litigation cost? Will there be a possibility of a counterclaim thereby exposing the client to damages? Can the money to be spent on litigation be put to better use in non-litigation efforts to protect the intellectual property or to gain a market advantage over competitors in the sector?

*Lesson: Move the client away from binary decision-making.*

## Tool No. 5: Slow down the Runaway Decision-Making Train

The lawyer can, and should, act as a brake for clients who want to make hasty decisions. While some decisions must be made on the spot, many can be delayed for more thoughtful consideration. So, what do you do when the client barks "We must decide now!"

### Tell and Show

What are the cognitive issues going on? According to J. Keith Murnighan and John C. Mowen in their book, "*The Art of High Stakes Decision Making: Tough Calls in a Speed Drive World*," the following occurs when clients make time pressured decisions.

➢ They increase their information processing speed but critically decrease the amount of information they consider.

*Result*: Bad decision because they shut themselves off from a broader perspective on what they should consider and what they need to decide.

➢ They increase their use of simpler rather than more sophisticated decision-making models.

*Result*: Bad decision because some decisions require a more thoughtful and detailed approach.

- ➢ They lock in on and defend their first chosen decision.

  *Result*: Bad decision because they fail to consider viable options.

They explain that this is why the Space Shuttle Challenger exploded on January 28, 1986, just 78 seconds after liftoff, causing the death of all seven astronauts. There was concern that certain equipment (called the "O-rings") might malfunction as a result. But those in charge said, essentially, "the whole world is watching; we must launch today!" This time-pressured decision inverted the normal decision-making process from the thoughtful, "Can you prove that it is safe to launch, because if you can't, we're not," to the reckless, "Can you show me launching isn't safe, because if you can't, we're launching!" Disaster ensued.

***Checklist to Slow Down***

- ☑ Ask, "if we had twice as much time to make this decision, would it be the same decision?"
- ☑ Ask "Yes, Option A can get to your goal but are there other options such as X or Y or Z that could get you there?"
- ☑ Ask a positive/negative question, "While there is certainly a need to make a prompt decision, should we consider (other options) or (discuss additional considerations) or (get input from other constituencies)?

***By Way of Illustration:***

Professor Maslanka was representing a company with locations in several states. Joe CEO wanted to fire an executive in the Tulsa location and to fire him "Now!" Neither he nor the General Counsel (GC) thought a quick decision was wise; after all, the executive had an employment contract and a rushed termination might violate it, exposing the client to a knotty lawsuit entailing substantial exposure. The GC and he hopped on a Zoom call with the CEO. Maslanka then launched into a lecture to the CEO on all the reasons why a quick firing was a bad idea. The GC lightly touched his arm, and she said "Joe do you remember that sophisticated equipment we bought a few years ago, and all the meetings, contract reviews, and negotiations that went into it? Well, that was a million-dollar decision and so is this one. And as you remind us "measure twice, cut once." Decision making slowed down, and the executive's contract was bought out at a discounted amount.

We tell you this war story because it illuminates effective counseling by the GC in the face of her client's rush to make a hasty decision. Let's deconstruct what she did:

- She reminded; she didn't lecture. No one likes to be told what to do as Professor Maslanka attempted.
- She told a short story, didn't she? Just like the story telling discussed in Section I.
- She used a quote that is, "measure twice, cut once." Quotes are effective because they are short, condense a lot into a small package, and carry the weight of the message you want delivered.

These types of quotes are called "aphorisms", which is defined as a "a pithy observation that contains a general truth." Aphorisms can do the heavy lifting of client communication. Consider how long it would take to explain to the client that it is advisable to take time to make a good decision versus, "measure twice, cut once."

*Lesson: Communicate with stories.*

### FINDING YOUR VOICE

While homemade quotes (from family, friends, mentors) are some of the best, here are other resources for you to explore:

- *The Oxford Dictionary of American Legal Quotations by Fred R. Shapiro*
- *The Quotable Lawyer by Tony Lyons*
- *The Little Black Book of Lawyer's Wisdom by Tony Lyons*

Research aphorisms that you think would work in your practice. One that was used by Professor Maslanka in explaining the cost of a lawsuit is from Voltaire, "There are only two times in my life I went broke. The first time is when I lost a lawsuit and the second time is when I won one."

## Tool No. 6: Listen for Phrases Portending Trouble

Counseling is about talking *and* listening. And what clients tell you gives a window into their true thinking.

### Tell and Show

Professor Maslanka is a big fan of noir detective fiction. So, on this tool he takes his cue from novelist Doug J. Swanson whose protagonist is Dallas private investigator Jack Flippo. This is from his novel "96 Tears":

> Jack thought about big nasty surprises, how they shouldn't happen. Not if you asked all the right questions, not if you paid attention. You only had to be one to alert for the signs. . . see it coming. That was the trick.

So here are several phrases that should put you on guard. Be alert when you hear them coming from clients or prospective clients.

- **Phrase No. 1: "Isn't it obvious?"**

What does this phrase signal?

- This signals an impatient client/prospective client.
- Clients/prospective clients often say this when they lack evidence to back up a claim. It is a sign that they are asserting a conclusion knowing they have nothing to back it up if pressed.
- Clients/prospective clients may use this to deflect a deeper inquiry into the facts of a matter.

Before responding though, determine if this is just meta talk to fill silence by a nervous client/prospective client or perhaps there is a genuine misunderstanding between the two of you (after all it is human nature that what is obvious to one person is not always obvious to another). But if not, then consider the following responses:

- Force them to elaborate. Ask, "Could you walk me through the evidence?"
- State, "Well the other side is going to drill down on this point. So, let's do it now."

➢ **Phrase No. 2: "This is a no-lose case. Guaranteed verdict!"**

What does this phrase signal?

➢ "He who maketh haste to be rich shall not be innocent." Proverbs 28:20. Some prospective clients are looking for a pay day. Period. Model Rule 3.1: Meritorious Claims and Contentions requires that you not take on a frivolous claim. Be wary.

➢ Drill down on how many lawyers this person has seen before seeing you. Chances are there were several, and the prospective client is trying to hook you on as a result of earlier rejections.

➢ Unrealistic expectations fueled by media accounts of large verdicts.

Consider the following responses:

➢ Explain there is much outside of your or their control—the judge assigned, the jury pool, how hard the party opposite will fight

➢ Discuss the small set of cases which result in large verdicts.

In addition, there are other phrases you should be attuned to, such as:

➢ **Phrase No. 3: "Everybody else is doing it."**

An invitation for the lawyer to engage in unethical conduct. "My competitor does not pay overtime to her employees so why should I" or "I'm sure the other side is not producing all of its documents in this lawsuit, so it is only fair that we not produce all of ours."

➢ **Phrase No. 4: "We've always thought about XYZ this way, so why should we change now?"**

A locked in client can be a dangerous client. Finger wagging from a lawyer seldom works, but a well-placed quote from a third person might start to turn the tide. A favorite of Professor Maslanka's is when Justice Frankfurter was criticized for changing his mind on a legal issue. His retort: "Wisdom too often never comes, and so one ought not to reject it merely because it comes late." *Henslee v. Union Planters Bank*, 335 U.S. 595 (1948). Feel free to leverage a quote.

*Lesson: Psychologists label these types of phrases as "leakage." The client is telling you what they're thinking indirectly. Pay attention.*

## Tool No. 7: Perform a Pre-Mortem

This is basically engaging in prospective hindsight; that is, looking forward to imagined disaster from a decision made today, as opposed to looking backwards on a decision already made that went wrong.

### Tell and Show

This invaluable counseling tool was perfected by research psychologist Gary Klein. He reasoned that doing a postmortem on a decision (what we call an after-action report) was only half of an idea. Why not ask the client—*before* a decision is implemented—the following question: "Imagine we implemented our decision. Imagine further that it crashed and burned. Let us ask ourselves why this could happen."

He suggests that all members of the decision-making team, lawyers included, be given two minutes to think of their top answer and having them each, in turn, relay it. (We suggest that you go from least senior to more senior in order to facilitate open and honest communication.) So much more effective than "It looks like we made a decision so does anyone see any problems?" Chances are there will be crickets. Klein writes that, "The pre-mortem reverses this (typical) dynamic."

*Lesson: Think different.*

## Tool No. 8: Know the Client's Communication Style

There are different tools to determine client's communication style as well as yours. One is called the Birkman and is described in an enlightening book, "*The Birkman Method: Your Personality at Work*" by Sharon Birkman Fink and Stephanie Capparell. You are one of four communication styles denoted by a color: red, yellow, green, blue.

How do you know your communication style? Take this test.

Rate *each* of the four phrases after the following five statements on the following scale:

6=the word or phrase that best describes you.
4=the phrase next most like you,
3=the phrase next most like you, and
1 =the phrase least descriptive of you.

Example:
I am likely to impress others as:

[4] A. Results Oriented
[6] B. Relationship Oriented
[1] C. Practical Oriented
[3] D. Action Oriented

I am likely to impress others as:
[___] A. Results Oriented.
[___] B. Relationship Oriented.
[___] C. Practical Oriented.
[___] D. Action Oriented.

The work I enjoy *most* is:
[___] A. Results-oriented so that time and effort spent is justified.
[___] B. Stimulating and thought-provoking with people I enjoy.
[___] C. Well planned, organized, and with a clear purpose.
[___] D. Challenging and likely to contribute something new.

My time is important, so I want to make sure that:
[___] A. What I do shows results today.
[___] B. My decisions and actions are meaningful and have long-term value.
[___] C. I plan carefully and follow the plan efficiently.
[___] D. I select activities that are the most interesting and important to me.

I feel *most* satisfied when I:
[___] A. Get more done than originally planned.
[___] B. Am in a position to help a friend.
[___] C. Solve a problem by collecting information and thinking it through.,
[___] D. Can come up with a new idea to meet a challenge.

I enjoy it when others see me as:
[___] A. A person who can be counted on to get things done.
[___] B. Someone who is trustworthy, sensitive, and creative.
[___] C. Someone who is organized and efficient.
[___] D. A person who loves a challenge.

| ADD THE TOTALS FOR EACH | A = [___] | B = [___] | C = [___] | D = [___] |
|---|---|---|---|---|
| Circle Your Highest Score | Red | Blue | Yellow | Green |

If you want to take the entire Birkman test for yourself, go to *www.birkman.com* and click "Get Started" followed by "I am interested in the Birkman for family or personal use." There is a modest fee associated with the test, so be aware before signing up.

When we first meet a client, or are just getting to know then, seconds count. We don't change who we are, but we do focus on who they are and communicate accordingly. Here's a summary chart on the traits of each color.

| | Red | Green | Yellow | Blue |
|---|---|---|---|---|
| **Office Hints** | Formal arrangement hones/ achievements work stacked by type | Individual style, motivational items, chaos, very disorganized | Functional job-related items, neat, very organized | Casual, open about family, personal items, lots of paper |
| **Body Language** | Direct eye contact, businesslike, firm handshake | Solid eye contact, friendly, smiles, easily broad gestures | Indirect eye contact, slow to smile, closed gestures | Variable eye contact, warm, casual, open gestures |
| **Speaking Style** | Direct, decisive, short, conversations, interrupts, to the point | Spontaneous, general, tells stories, jokes, talks more than listens | Deliberate, slow, organized, logical, asked detailed questions | Thoughtful, casual, stories, questions, suggestions |
| **Expectations** | Results, bottom-like, frankness, efficiency | Creativity, enthusiasm, innovation, novelty, adventure | Thoroughness, detail, systematic accuracy, logic | Relationships, trust, loyalty, friendship, personal |
| **Focus Strength** | Objectives, pragmatic, confident, assertive | Ideas, imaginative, creative, enthusiastic, unorganized, unrealistic, impractical | Process objective, analytical, thorough, rigid, indecisive, impersonal | Feelings of empathy, loyalty, trustworthy, persuasive, overly sensitive, internalizes and avoids conflicts |
| **Best Approach** | Short conversation, begin with results, provide choices, be direct, conciseness | Allow time to talk, show enthusiasm, listen and discuss new ideas, use testimonials | Provide written information, allow time to review history or experience, expect detailed questions | Face-to-face is essential to get to know them, relationship, discuss needs |
| **Decision-Making** | Will decide on the spot if information supports decision | Will decide on the spot if the level of enthusiasm is high | Will rarely decide quickly. Needs a chance to review information and consider the decision. | Will rarely decide quickly. Needs a chance to get to know you. |

All of this is helpful in meeting a client's communication needs.

*Lesson: The true value of a communication style test is not so much your style, but in helping you to understand the client's style. Remember: it's always about the client.*

**FINDING YOUR VOICE**

Take a recently concluded matter from your practice or, if you are a student, from a competition packet for mock trial or other advocacy competition. Write an after-action report for your client, identifying practical steps they can take moving forward, to lessen or eliminate the risk of a similar problem. Consider what you know about the client. Should your report get right to the point, or use examples and analogies? Should it be blunt and direct, or more circumspect? Should you start by spending time on what went well, or use B.L.U.F.?

## II. MAINTAINING EFFECTIVE COMMUNICATION

### The Challenge: How Do I Handle Tough Conversations?

As with the start of any relationship, the commencement of an ACR is full of promise and good vibes. But reality inevitably intervenes. So, bad news must be delivered, client objectives reassessed, losses explained. And Model Rule 1.4: Communication requires that clients be "reasonably informed about the status of the matter." This includes bad news. While we are professionals, we are also human. We seek to avoid or put off these discussions. Consider the following tools in overcoming these temptations.

### Tool No. 1: Avoid Ego

Move away from an adversarial mindset.

## Tell and Show

If a person responds with personal attacks, recognize that the person is equating your raising of the thorny issue with you being rude or out of line. You are not being rude; you are being professional and responsible. An ACR's focus must always be on the needs of the client, not on the needs of the lawyer. If a client reacts badly to bad news, it is never about you but about the bad news. It's about anger transference. Do not make it about yourself by being defensive. Remember that you are in 0% control of what the client says or does, but in 100% control of what you say or do in response.

*Lesson: Continue to educate yourself on this point. Check out Ryan Holiday's insightful book, "Ego is the Enemy: The fight to master our greatest opponent." Well worth the time.*

### The Neurodiversity Insight

Avoid putting the onus on the neurodivergent individual client or colleague. Instead of expecting a neurodivergent person to adjust to the neurotypical, try being the one who adjusts your expectations, especially in the social context. Shawntal Mallory, Executive Director of the Nebraska Legal Diversity Counsel writes, "I am consistently serious about two main things—mindfulness and action. In constantly strategizing about inclusion issues, I have often been asked, 'where can I begin in my journey to help make a difference?' "

If a client asks you to repeat something, slow down, or explain something again, then do it and don't take it personally.

You do not have to disclose to a client that you are neurodivergent, and you should not expect a client to disclose to you. Second, you do not have to mask. Being neurodivergent is not a problem to be solved. You do have to prepare for the client interaction. All lawyers can improve their communication skills, hence this book. There is no one right way to communicate so the best strategies are the ones that work with you and for you depending on the circumstances.

## Tool No. 2: Jettison Jargon

We are used to speaking in the language of our peers; that is, the language of other lawyers. But lawyer talk is a foreign language to our clients.

### Tell and Show

Instead of using legal jargon and complex terms, use straightforward language without oversimplifying. The structure should be logical and organized. Start with setting up the context and giving the most important information first, then giving the details.

Lawyers tend to camouflage bad news through resorting to jargon that makes perfect sense to lawyers but is foreign to clients. MR 1.4 (b) mandates that we "shall explain a matter to the extent reasonably necessary to permit the client to make informed decision regarding the representation" which presupposes that we speak to clients in a "language" they can understand.

Which of these options do you think a client would find most understandable?

***Option A:***

"We are about to begin the discovery phase of this lawsuit, where the other side learns of the documents and information that the other side will rely upon."

Or,

***Option B:***

"We're entering the discovery phase of this litigation and will propound interrogatories, request for production, request for admissions. Once completed, we'll then deteremine what types of depositions are most suitable for further discovery."

*Lesson: Always speak to people in a language they can understand.*

**The Neurodiversity Insight**

Communicate clearly and unambiguously. This sounds obvious but lawyers tend to get caught up in our own expertise and knowledge and forget that our listeners are not legal experts. Things like using legal jargon and abbreviations, being sarcastic, and failing to provide context show a lack of consideration for the client and what is in their best interest.

You might be thinking, *everyone* uses "escheat". Ask yourself, why is it so important that you use it? Are you trying to establish your expertise or intelligence? The best way to do that is not by making other people feel inadequate or unable to understand what you are saying.

Something as innocuous as "I need this document soon," or "let's talk about this later," is subjective. Instead, saying "I need this document before the end of the business day" and "we can talk about this at 3pm," are clear and unambiguous.

Speak literally. You might think you do this but how many times have you said or heard, "do you have a second/minute?" Is that really what you mean? What you mean is that you need to speak with the person for a short period of time, so say that: "Do you have 10 minutes to answer a question?"

From a neurodivergent perspective, neurotypical individuals do not always say what they mean. Here's an example:

Neurotypical person says, "We're going to get coffee."

Someone with autism will respond, "Ok, have fun."

Neurotypical person thinks, "Why doesn't she want to come with us?"

Neurodivergent person thinks, "Why are you telling me this, don't you want me to come?"

Instead of assuming people will pick up on social cues, ensure a shared understanding by stating the mutual goal. "We're going to get coffee, would you like to join us?"

## Tool No. 3: Embrace Clarity

Communication consultant Holly Weeks writes in her article "Taking the Stress Out of Stressful Conversations" that there is a DNA to managing hard conversations. Part of that DNA is clarity in communication. She advises us to avoid euphemisms or talking in circles. She writes:

"Under strained circumstances, we all tend to shy away from clarity because we equate it with brutality. . . Yet there's nothing inherently brutal about honesty. It is not the content but the delivery of the news that makes it brutal or humane. Ask a surgeon; ask a priest; ask a cop. If a message is given skillfully—even though the news is bad—the content may still be tolerable."

Our advice: treat a client as a responsible adult and they will generally respond as responsible adults.

### Tell and Show

Which is clearer, Option A or Option B:

***Option A:***

Lawyer explains to Client: "We received an electronic transmission from the court clerk, granting in full the other side's Motion for Failure to State a Claim pursuant to Rule 12(b)(6). A formal order from the court will follow in due course."

***Option B:***

Lawyer explains to Client: "Recall that the person we are suing filed a request with the court to dismiss your claim because it does not identify a violation of contract law. We fought it but the judge disagreed with our argument and dismissed your lawsuit today. We will have a chance to refile the lawsuit based on new facts but that will be a long shot.

*Lesson: Lighten the client's cognitive processing load.*

## Tool No. 4: Rolling out the Spikes

Those in the medical profession have conversations about addressing difficult topics with patients, and most medical schools have entire courses dedicated to patient communication. One common method used by doctors when delivering bad news is the S.P.I.K.E.S. protocol designed by Dr. Walter F. Baile when he was a physician and professor at the University of Texas MD Anderson Cancer Center.

### Tell and Show

S.P.I.K.E.S. stands for Setting up, Perception, Invitation, Knowledge, Emotions with empathy, and Strategy or Summary. Although delivering bad medical news is not identical to the bad news lawyers may have to communicate, the underlying premise is the same.

**S**etting Up: mentally rehearse and prepare for the client's response. Although the conversation may be upsetting or disappointing, the client needs the information to make informed decisions and move forward.

**P**erception: the client's perception of the news can help you determine how to convey the information. What does the client know about the case or project, and what do they understand so far? If you do not know what the client's perception is, you can ask questions to get a sense of it. This can also help you determine if, despite your ongoing communication, the client's expectations are unrealistic.

**I**nvitation: Obtaining the client's invitation means finding out ahead of time how much and the best way to communicate tough information. Some clients want a scheduled conference, some written memos. Some want calls at the start or end of the work day. Find out.

**K**nowledge: Giving knowledge and information to the client at the start of the conversation, not hedging or trying to bury the lead. Try: "Unfortunately, I have some bad news. . ."; "I have some difficult news to deliver"; or "This next phase will be expensive, so I'd like to talk about it." Not all difficult conversations are bad news. Many are about budget, expert costs, trial costs, etc. Instead of it being a shock, a preview allows the client a moment to process and prepare for what you are going to tell them.

Emotions with empathy: Address the client's emotions with empathetic responses. You cannot predict how every client will react, but you can be prepared to give them space for it.

Strategy or Summary: Having a clear plan alleviates uncertainty and gives the client options and agency, even when that plan is potentially ending the attorney-client relationship or settling for a low dollar amount because going to trial is too risky or too expensive.

***By Way of Illustration:***

Here is an example of what a S.P.I.K.E.S. Protocol conversation might look like:

> *Lawyer:* I'm sorry to say that the judge has issued her decision, and it is not in our favor. She has granted the defendant's motion for summary judgment. Do you remember our conversation in February about the motion for summary judgment and what that is?
>
> *Client:* Sort of but what does that mean?
>
> *Lawyer:* It means that [define]. I know this is not what we wanted the outcome to be, I wish the news was better.
>
> *Client:* Oh no! That is not fair! Does that mean we lose? Is the case over?
>
> *Lawyer:* Unfortunately, it does mean the case is over. There is an option to appeal the judge's decision to the appellate court, but this is not a decision you should make right at this moment. The costs are [range of money], and the chances of winning are [give percentage of reversal]. The deadline to file a notice of appeal is [date] and there is a filing fee as well as the cost for the attorney's time to draft it. My advice is to take a few days to think about it before deciding.

*Client:* I don't need to think about it. The judge is wrong, and we need to appeal or file a complaint. Can't we call the bar and complain about the other attorney?

*Lawyer:* I understand where you are coming from, and it is frustrating. The course of action is an appeal and one reason there is a 30-day deadline for filing the notice to appeal is to allow time to decide if it is a reasonable path to pursue.

*Client:* I am the one who is wronged here. If we don't appeal, that means it's over.

*Lawyer:* That is correct, and it is a lot to take in, especially as this has been more than a year-long process.

*Client:* So, file the appeal. I know I am in the right, and we should win.

*Lawyer:* Very briefly, here is what an appeal is like. I've done some preliminary research. [Give statistics and legal analysis.] There is no guarantee we would win an appeal and if we did that does not mean you win the case. It means we'd come back to the trial court and keep going forward with the case. The defendant would be more open to settling but you would have incurred more costs. We can certainly go forward with an appeal, but I want you to fully understand what that entails, including the time and money costs. I do think it is best to give it at least a day or two before making such a big decision. Why don't I contact you next week after you've had some time to process the benefits and costs?

In this scenario, the lawyer states the issue right away and sticks to the facts and the lawyer does not join in blaming individuals. The lawyer keeps their own emotions in check while acknowledging their client's emotions. The lawyer can't give the client what they want but can show understanding and transparency.

*Lesson: Don't be concerned about sounding smart; be concerned about sounding being understood.*

## The Challenge: How Do I Communicate with Clients Different from Me?

According to the United States Census Bureau, as of 2022, there are 45,000,000 Americans with limited English proficiency (LEP) and approximately 47% of those are immigrants with LEP.

We live in a diverse society, and to be a competent lawyer, you must be able to communicate with clients from varying backgrounds, with varying cognitive proficiencies. You must be sensitive to these differences, whether they are based on gender, neurodiversity, or culture.

## Tool No. 1: Understand Your Own Implicit Bias

Each of us, the authors of this book included, has implicit bias. Bias means prejudice in favor of or against one thing, person, or group. Implicit means that it is unconscious, our brains tend to automatically do it. When we understand our implicit bias and stop trying to force clients into our way of communicating, and acknowledge their way of communicating, we become effective counselors.

### Tell and Show

Not understanding your implicit bias makes you an ineffective counselor because you skip over the facts regarding your client. When you understand your implicit bias, it forces you to go back and ask yourself what facts support that notion. It means that you treat each client as an individual.

***By Way of Illustration:***

A lawyer may have a general belief that Asians tend to be studious. Perhaps this general belief applies to your client, but not necessarily. If this is an important fact in their legal issue, you need to recognize that your belief may be based on unsubstantiated assumptions not particularized facts.

Putting aside our implicit bias is a challenge to put into practice because, as we alluded to previously, and as Daniel Kahneman explains, our brains make quick, automatic judgments about others (Type 1 thinking). Our instinct is to think of these cognitive shortcuts as right judgments because it's easier. But these presumptions are frequently erroneous because they are based on our limited and, often, non-culturally diverse experiences.

One variation of this is confirmation bias, in which we unconsciously seek information that confirms our pre-existing beliefs. We want to be "right" about what we believe so our brains search for things to confirm this and ignore information counter to this.

If someone draws attention to your potential bias, be careful not to shift into a self-preservation mode. They might just be right. And feel free to ask clarifying questions to better understand your potential bias. Be candid and honest with yourself. This will make you a better counselor. There is an implicit-association bias test from Harvard. It was introduced in scientific literature in 1998. Take it by going to implicit.harvard.edu.

*Lesson: It is all too human to believe that we are different people than reality allows.*

**FINDING YOUR VOICE**

One way to begin to discover and enter into a culture is to read books by authors who hail from that culture or place, such as *The Kite Runner* by Khaled Hosseini, or *Half of a Yellow Sun* by Chimimanda Ngozi Adichie. If your practice serves particular cultural groups, or you intend to do so, compile a reading list from that part of the world. Not unlike time spent on a trip abroad, you may find interesting perspectives, challenging ideas, cultural norms that differ from yours. A single book is but a window but may also give you a talking point when you are one-on-one with your clients. Professor LeBoeuf found the poet Pablo Neruda to be a great entry point for conversations with her Chilean-born son-in-law, if only to hear arguments about which English translation is best.

**The Neurodiversity Insight**

If your client has disclosed, or you suspect, they are neurodivergent or have a disability, recognize whether your initial thoughts are actually biases based on lack of knowledge: e.g., concerns about competence or ability to understand. A better approach is to presume competence and treat the client as you would anyone else, with respect and empathy.

Regardless of whether someone is neurotypical or neurodivergent, different people have different communication styles. While some neurodivergent individuals may rely less on non-verbal cues or tone of voice when communicating, just as many are very expressive. Pay attention to how your client responds to you and whether they seem uncomfortable or confused.

What you do notice is when someone diverges. For example, if someone does not make eye contact, we might think they are not paying attention to ourselves. Like the cognitive biases addressed in cultural competency, there is a cognitive bias to prefer people like us. We have embedded social norms, and we feel safer in conformity; when someone is like you, there is less you must try to predict or figure out about them. It takes additional cognitive effort to understand somebody different. Perhaps ironically, neurodivergent individuals put in this additional effort all the time, so that they are not perceived differently. This is why it is important to challenge our default approach and ask ourselves, "why am I doing it this way, is this the only way to do it?"

Ask what communication style the client prefers or what works best for them. This does not mean you should ask if they are neurodivergent (never do that). You do not have to know if someone is neurodivergent to ask what communication style works best for them. It is not ableist to do this, it is proactive and perhaps even necessary for you to provide competent representation.

## Tool No. 2: Speak to People in a Language They Can Understand

Odds are, you will represent clients whose native language is not English (think back to the 2022 U.S. Census). Your duty is to figure out if you need a translator to communicate with your client.

This duty is anchored in ABA Model Rule 1.4: "Communications," which places the burden of effective communication where it belongs—on the lawyer. This burden is explained in ABA Formal Opinion 500 (October 6, 2021), "Language Access in the Client-Lawyer Relationship."

### Tell and Show

When you strip away all its lawyer-like euphemisms, Opinion 500's message is very direct: Lawyers must adapt to their clients' communication needs, not the other way around.

In fulfilling your ethical duties on language access, there are two questions you must ask yourself:

- ➢ **Does the client adequately comprehend my communications?**

It is your duty as a lawyer to ensure that the answer is "yes." What if you and the client speak a common language but the client is more fluent?

Even if you have some language fluency, the inquiry does not end. You must next determine whether your background and life experiences are sufficient to attribute meaning to a client's behavior, expressions, and cultural experiences. Literal translation is not enough, as some concepts and ideas are simply lost in translation.

- ➢ **What are the measures that must be taken to establish communication?**

You might consider using a client's friend or family member as a translator. This is inadvisable.

When a friend or family member assists with your communications, confidentiality is lost. Moreover, because of the relationship, the friend or family member might have a personal interest or self-interest in the information being translated. This creates a temptation to distort or alter communication between the client and the lawyer. Bottom line, this solution is what ABA Opinion 500 describes as "ethically fraught."

Instead, exercise due diligence in hiring a qualified interpreter. Per ethical obligations under ABA Model Rule 1.1: "Competence," hiring a translator is no different for the lawyer than hiring any other professional to assist in representation. The due diligence questions are modified, but still essentially the same:

- What is your educational background?
- What is your experience in translating legal matters?
- Do you have any language proficiency certifications?
- Do you understand the client's culture?

Reminder: Language is fluid! There are differences by country, and even by region in the same country. The person who can best assist in asking these questions, and, therefore, in hiring a competent translator, is your client.

Another less favored option is the use of a multilingual lawyer or staff member in a lawyer's office. You must proceed "cautiously" if utilizing this option because you may not be competent enough to assess an associate lawyer or staff's level of proficiency in that language. Lawyers like this option because it's convenient for them, but it may not be in the client's best interest. Remember: many languages use various dialects, with shaded and nuanced differences. The law is a formal proceeding, and the necessity of precision does not evaporate because of the need for translation.

*Leson: Communication involves more than mere language.*

### The Neurodiversity Insight

Auditory processing delay affects the brain's ability to process and interpret sounds. The person is not hard of hearing, but they struggle to manage the information they hear. Similar to auditory sensitivity, auditory processing delay makes it hard to filter out irrelevant sensory information or to filter out background noises. Very simply, it hears all noises at the same volume and cannot focus on the sounds that matter. For example, if you are in a client meeting and there is a wall clock in the room, someone with auditory sensitivity would hear the tick-tock at the same level as your voice.

It's not realistic to remove all background noises. Instead, be patient and give people a little time to process the conversation. For example, at the end of a client meeting, instead of saying, "any questions," show that you understand the person might need time to process the discussion by saying, "why don't you think through our discussion and email me your questions." Or you can offer to follow up with an email in a day or two to see if there are any questions.

## The Challenge: How Do I Prepare a Client for Litigation?

Litigation is stressful. Clients on both sides of a lawsuit may feel a great deal of mental and emotional stress, worrying about unknown outcomes and other uncertainties such as cost. It is often difficult for a client to sit by, while someone else learns the facts of their matter, questions what they did and why, and argues their case. It is equally difficult for clients when they are under pressure to perform in the deposition room and on the stand, where the environment and rules are unfamiliar.

Prepared clients know what to expect at each stage of litigation, are given the information they need to evaluate the risks and benefits of proceeding, and are provided frequent opportunities to ask questions and to express their concerns in a safe and responsive environment.

## Tool No. 1: Provide Continuous Updates

Lessen the intensity by providing regular updates as the case or project progresses, including why it isn't progressing if that is the case. This allows you to revisit and adjust expectations incrementally instead of dropping a huge bomb. Continually revisit the alignment (or lack of) between legal principles and your actions, on the one hand, and the client's expectations, on the other.

### Tell and Show

Ever hear of catastrophic thinking? Here's a definition: it is a cognitive distortion where a person assumes the worst possible outcome of a situation, distorting minor problems into a disaster. Clients who are sued often engage in this type of thinking. Help them with one of the following techniques:

- Periodically, communicate with them on the status of the lawsuit.
- Explain, from time to time, that nothing is happening in their lawsuit and that this is not unusual. (But don't charge for this.)
- Manage expectations and provide realistic scenarios from the outset of the ACR.

*Lesson: When in doubt, overly communicate.*

## Tool No. 2: Teach the Litigation Lifecycle

You are watching a game in a country you never visited before now. You have never seen this game played. But you can see there is a ball, three teams, and shifting alliances among the players. The game is a fast one. You're not really sure why the audience is shouting or cheering. And although you can see a net that seems to be the end goal, there is a lot of play that does not involve the net but still leads to shouts or cheers. When do you get excited? Who is winning? What are the rules? You have a local friend sitting next to you explaining the action on the fly, but it isn't really making sense, and you don't have the big picture. How do you feel?

## Tell and Show

Legal clients are observers of a game whose rules they do not fully understand. One day their lawyers are cheering, the next day they are disappointed. Should the client be encouraged or discouraged? Is their claim "winning" or "losing"? Much of what the client hears is couched in maybes: It could go this way, but it could go that; this could be a good sign, but maybe not; we will have to wait and see what happens next. Your client wants to know some very specific things. Are we winning, or not? When is it time to get worried? What is happening right now?

You may think you can give a few explanations, and the client will get it. You may think your business-savvy, educated, engaged client already knows what you do. On both counts, you are likely wrong. From the very beginning of your retention as counsel, all the way through the end of the case, it is truly important to repeatedly describe the life cycle of a lawsuit, and where the client is now in that cycle. From initiation through discovery through motions practice and, eventually, trial, you will know and understand the long periods of quiet, the times when the case gets exceptionally busy, the meaning and purpose of the steps being taken. Your client, most assuredly, will not understand all of that.

***By Way of Illustration:***

Clients should be informed that the early part of the case involves discovery, and what that entails. What, for instance, is a request for admission? They should know that it may take some time to conduct discovery, and which parts they will be involved with. By way of illustration, you may want them to help you prepare for their opponent's deposition, and to be present. Clients should be told that it will likely be necessary in the discovery phase to involve the court in ironing out disputes. And clients should be told that, for the most part, months may go by when from their perspective it seems like "nothing" is happening. They should also be told that they will be expected to give discovery and what they can do now, to preserve documents and information, and to gather what is relevant for your review.

In discussing the life cycle of a case, it is a good idea to have discussions with the client about how much contact they want, and whether they prefer to receive updates by telephone or email. Setting up these expectations early avoids misunderstandings and conflicts later.

*Lesson: Often, the greatest challenge of lawyering is remembering that there was a time when you did not know something. Apply this wisdom to communicating with your client.*

## Tool No. 3: Dispel Myths of Deposition Testimony

In preparing a client to comminate via sworn testimony, lawyers too often take an overly simplistic approach, limiting their counsel to "tell the truth." Reality though tells us that clients are operating under many misperceptions. Here are their Myths and the Myth Busters.

### Tell and Show

Clear and effective communication often means bringing into the open unspoken beliefs that drive behavior. These unspoken beliefs can be traps that put the client in an unfavorable position, leading them to testify poorly. Be aware of the unspoken drivers of your client's behavior throughout the litigation process. Discussed and examined, these influences can be set aside in favor of a better approach. Communicating advice in punchy ways will help with witness recall, yielding good results.

***Myth: "If I tell them what happened, this will all be over."***

Litigants often think, in their heart of hearts, that if they just tell their story the case will be resolved. Preparing a client for deposition means addressing this misleading belief out loud.

***Myth Buster: Nobody ever stood up in the middle of taking a deposition and said, "Oh my gosh, I had no idea! Let me get my checkbook. Who should I make the check to?"***

Naming this myth out loud makes a client laugh, yes, but is also memorable. Points that stick result in changed behavior.

When a client acknowledges that the case will not screech to a halt no matter how well they advocate (your job), as opposed to discussing the facts known to them (their job), they can focus on the hard work of being a witness, which is a big enough job in itself.

***Myth: "The written word is more important than the spoken word"***

Remind people out loud that the spoken word is evidence. This fact may be intuitive to those who are regularly in a courtroom but is not intuitive to the lay person. Time after time, witnesses say, "this happened, but I have no proof of it."

***Myth Buster: Yes, you do have proof! You have your testimony.***

Bolsters to witness credibility may exist separately, or they may not: a calendar entry, a ticket stub, another person's testimony. But testimony is evidence, and it is evidence that matters, so prepare your client to come fully prepared to state the facts, unconcerned about what may or may not be in writing. That's for later.

***Myth: "If it's in writing it must be true"***

The flip side of this instinctive preference for written documents is the thought that what is in writing must be true. Shown someone else's draft, email, or memorandum, the unprepared witness may presume its contents are accurate,and testify accordingly, even when the document does not fit their own story line or knowledge of what happened. Clients must be taught to be skeptical, to read before speaking, to question the authenticity of anything in writing, and to refrain from speaking to someone else's intent. Without this preparation, they are more likely than not to conform their testimony to whatever is in writing, true or not.

***Myth Buster: Using documents that you know contradict or vary from your client's testimony ask, "Is this correct? Do you agree?"***

If not, have the Client practice saying out loud that it's wrong, and how they know.

### *Myth: "If my lawyer wrote it, it must be right!"*

A corollary to the idea that a written document must be accurate is the idea that whatever a lawyer puts in writing must be "right." Nope. Unless this myth is addressed out loud, your client might very well feel caught between championing what you wrote (reasoning that it must be "legally correct"), and telling the facts as they know them. Arm them ahead of time with how to address this puzzle. Your client should know you have no pride of authorship. When it comes to sworn testimony, the truth is all that counts. And they should know that the sky will not fall when mistakes are acknowledged. To the contrary, the acknowledgement may bolster credibility.

### *Myth Buster: Even lawyers make mistakes. It's a fact of litigation life.*

Our knowledge of a matter changes over time, as witnesses are interviewed or deposed, documents are located and produced, legal theories researched. It is inevitable that early drafts in a case may turn out to be less than perfect. An initial pleading may misstate facts; early discovery responses may be incomplete.

Put the client in the driver's seat. Have them practice a version of, "no that's not strictly accurate, here's what actually happened." Prepare them to answer the inevitable, "then why does it say that," with "you'll have to ask my lawyer" or "that's what we thought at the time, but we know better now."

### *Myth: "I don't have to remember now; I can testify about it later."*

The witness being deposed has one eye on the exit sign. And who can blame them? Never in our lives—not even when we are children—does another adult make us sit and concentrate on answering questions, one after another, with no right to get up and leave, and no ability to ask questions in return. Is it any wonder that the ingenuous witness finds a thousand ways to get to the exit? "I don't know" and "I don't remember" are at the top of the list.

### *Myth Buster: If you don't remember now, Judge won't let you remember later.*

The modern tribunal discourages trial by ambush. If your client wants to tell them what happened when it matters (at trial), they must fully answer questions at deposition, to the best of their ability. . . No matter how badly they would like to be finished with this process.

*Lesson: Preparing the client for deposition is a lot more than telling them, "Just tell the truth."*

## Tool No. 4: Dispel the Myths of Trial Testimony

As with deposition testimony, so too with trial testimony. Part of a lawyer's role in communicating with clients is educating them on how to effectively give trial testimony

### Tell and Show

Giving testimony in court is, in a strange way, both culturally familiar and personally unfamiliar to the average person. Oh sure, our clients and witnesses have seen courtroom dramas on YouTube, television, or at the cinema. But the ins and outs of establishing credibility while giving testimony? Or the way it feels to be the center of the entire room's attention, in a setting full of symbolism and unfamiliar language? New and new. Potential witnesses need more coaching regarding the courtroom and the process of testifying than they probably know. And here too they often have deeply held, unspoken beliefs that need to be pulled into the open and addressed. How and what you communicate can make a winning difference.

### *Myth: "The outcome depends on me."*

Every major religion focuses on letting go of the ego. Why? Because the ego drives us. Especially in western culture, raised on stories of self-determination and creative problem solving, we often believe we have greater influence and control than we do. The pressure on a witness, when they believe the outcome of a case is dependent entirely on their testimony—and they often do believe this—can have adverse effect. Too much pressure leads to problems such as freezing or forgetting testimony, rambling beyond the question, arguing rather than testifying, and speaking to matters that are better addressed by someone else with more direct or complete knowledge.

***Myth Buster: You are not the whole case.***

Documents and other witnesses will speak about things you cannot. If someone else addresses a fact they know well, and you relay it imperfectly because you only know it secondhand, your testimony will conflict, and the jury won't know who to believe. Cases are won and lost on credibility. Speak to what you directly saw, heard, read, or did, and leave the rest to other sources, including other witnesses.

In addition to streamlining the trial, this approach takes a burden from the witness that improves their ability to testify accurately and completely.

***Myth: "I should fight fire with fire!"***

Jurors differ from lawyers and litigants in a fundamental way. They are not immersed in the conflict before them and are conflict-averse. Unable to leave, and unable to distract themselves, they are right in the middle of the conflict in the courtroom. Verbal sparring, sarcasm, and bullying can all lead to juror discomfort. Discomfort can lead to tuning out.

***Myth Buster: Credibility and empathy are currency in jury trials.***

The jury listens best when they can put themselves in a witness's shoes. When a witness responds to aggressive questioning, sarcasm, and bullying by staying calm, giving clear and measured responses, and looking directly at the jury, jury sentiment will likely swing their way. Jurors can picture being in their shoes and imagine how they might respond to the aggression. But when the witness gives back as good as they got? Explain to the client that, while they may feel better, the jury will tune out, making grocery lists in their heads, fretting about work and kids, and counting minutes until the next break.

***Myth: "If Judge knows the truth, they will throw this case out."***

The person in the black robe, sitting at the center of the courtroom, has the most authority. . .right? We rise for them. We are silent when they speak. They make rulings and issue orders, decide when we will assemble and when we can leave. And yet, like branches of government, the jury and the judge each have roles that are sacrosanct and distinct. And once the jury trial is under way, the Judge is not the arbiter of the facts. Your clients and witnesses will not grasp this. Unschooled witnesses will address their testimony to the Judge, while a jury sits ignored in the box. And witnesses left to their own devices will try to be their own advocates, making emotional pleas and trying their hand at legal arguments you discussed with them in the privacy of your conference room.

***Myth Buster: You pay me a lot of money to be here. Let me do my job (advocacy), while you do yours (testifying to what you know). And your job is big enough.***

The job of the client on the stand is to answer the question with what they know. Teach your client to focus on the question. Do you understand every part of the question? Is this one question or several? Do you have personal knowledge? Focus on your answer. Are you answering the question, and only the question, one at a time?

Teach your witnesses to be in the moment and to address themselves to the jury. This is not normal conversation. This is a formalized, ritualized process, by which strangers to the controversy try to ferret out the facts and determine credibility. Witnesses must be trained in order to be effective.

***Myth: "The jury will instinctively know who is more credible."***

Not so. While juries do a pretty good job, unlike the parties themselves they do not have the benefit of years (or decades) of exposure to the facts and personalities involved. They can never know the full back story of the witnesses: who is a lifelong community volunteer or who cheated on exams in college. Juries have a day, a week, maybe a month, to learn the facts, understand the issues, and make credibility determinations about lawyers, witnesses, and parties. And they are doing all this in the context of both boredom and stress. They may not use their phones, consult Google or Gen AI, check work emails, take a walk to clear their heads, or determine their own lunch hour.

So, we must teach our witnesses to signal credibility, in every way possible. Yes, it is a learned skill.

***Myth Buster: A jury has nothing to look at but you and the other participants in the courtroom.***

Jurors are watching and listening for every sign of credibility, as they have been instructed that determining credibility is up to them alone. Look the jurors in the eye while testifying (but don't stare them down!). Sit up straight and try not to fidget or rock your chair. Speak clearly and slowly, into the microphone. Show respect to every person in the courtroom, even opposing counsel. Smile when appropriate or natural.

The more these rules are followed, the more likely the witness is to exude confidence, which also bolsters credibility.

***Myth: "I am powerless before the Judge and the lawyers."***

You told your witnesses not to argue with opposing counsel, and to show respect to the Judge, the jury, the lawyers, and the litigants in the courtroom. But are they powerless? Absolutely not. Witnesses have power and control over the most important thing—the questions they are asked. They are entitled to, and must, ask for clarification whenever appropriate. This will mean speaking up for themselves, a circumstance that many witnesses cannot imagine is "allowed." Empower them.

***Myth Buster: You are entitled to one question at a time. You are entitled to know exactly what you are answering. You are entitled to finish your answer.***

If you do not understand a word or a question, ask for clarification before you answer. If you did not fully hear the question, ask that it be repeated. If there was an objection and you don't know whether or not you can answer, ask the Judge or counsel if you can answer. If you forgot the question that was asked, ask for the question again. If you have not finished your answer, ask to complete it before answering the next question. If you need a break, or a tissue, or water. . . ask.

*Lesson: Always communicate to the client that—regardless of the trial outcome—life goes on. Lawyers communicate perspective.*

## III. ACR CONCLUSION (OR NOT)

### The Challenge: How Do I End an ACR?

Everything that has a beginning also has an ending. The ACR is no different. Effective communication is again paramount to successfully ending an ACR.

### Tool No. 1: The Disengagement Letter

What starts well, ends well. But the end only ends well if you communicate that the end has come. An effective way to communicate an ACR's conclusion is variously called a "Disengagement Letter" or a "Termination of Representation" letter. Labels don't matter. Instead, what matters is the letter's substance and the letter's tone.

As with any contractual relationship, it is best to memorialize in writing. But that is only half the equation. The other half is how to say what needs to be said.

#### Tell and Show

***By Way of Illustration:***

Here are some suggestions for drafting to make clear that the ACR is over:

**Suggestion 1:**

Consider going back to Bottom Line Up Front (B.L.U.F.): Start with Your B.L.U.F. in the opening paragraph:

> *Lawyer:* "I am pleased to inform you that our legal services regarding (brief description of the legal matter because there might be more than one) have been successfully concluded as of (date). We discussed this resolution on (date of discussion)."

**Suggestion 2:**

The next paragraph contemplates possible future events, providing an opportunity to reconfirm the closure of the matter.

> *Lawyer:* "Please note that any other legal issues related to this matter, or any new legal work, will require a new engagement letter for our services."

**Suggestion 3:**

What about the "tone"? Even if the outcome was not ideal, the tone must be professional.

> *Lawyer:* "While we wish the outcome had been more in align with your aspirations, we were honored to represent you and extend our heartfelt thanks for the trust you placed in us."

*Lesson: Every opportunity to communicate with the client is an opportunity to educate and to bond.*

## Tool No. 2: Remind Client of What Will Not Be Done

Recall that in forming an ACR, communication regarding what a lawyer will <u>not</u> be doing is just as important as stating what a lawyer <u>will</u> be doing. The same is true with the ending of the ACR.

### Tell and Show

Let's expand on what we reference in Tool No. 1. Comment 4 to Model Rule 1.3: Diligence says it best:

> Doubt about whether a client-lawyer relationship still exists should be clarified by the lawyer, preferably in writing, so that the client will not mistakenly suppose the lawyer is looking after the client's affairs when the lawyer has ceased to do so. For example, if a lawyer has handled a judicial or administrative proceeding that produced a result adverse to the client and the lawyer and the client have not agreed that the lawyer will handle the matter on appeal, the lawyer must consult with the client about the possibility of appeal before relinquishing responsibility for the matter.

*Lesson: This is a fitting conclusion on communicating with clients because it underscores, yet again, that it's always the lawyer's burden to communicate clearly to the client. Always.*

# CHAPTER 3

# PERSUADING

Our final section on communication deals with persuasion. While building upon Sections 1 and 2, we shift the focus in Section 3 to advocacy. Advocacy in the context of resolving disputes—whether through negotiation with counsel opposite, formal mediation, or trial and binding arbitration.

Persuasion is never accomplished when we lecture, sermonize or threaten. Indeed, the linguistic origins of "persuade" are diametrically opposite in meaning and intent to this ineffective trio. In Latin, "per" means "thoroughly, strongly" while "suade" means "urging in a sweet, pleasant manner." Persuasion for lawyers therefore consists of moving others to your client's positions through effective communication.

You'll see that effective communication here, as with the other sections, often focuses on human nature, cognitive theory, and interpersonal skills.

## I. RESOLUTION THROUGH NEGOTIATION

**The Challenge: How Do You Initiate a Resolution with a Party Opposite?**

With persuasion, communication comes in two flavors: words and actions. Messages can be delivered effectively through each or a combination of both.

**Tool No. 1: Avoid Demonizing the Party Opposite**

Conflict with the party opposite and their counsel is part of lawyering. But while conflict is inevitable, demonizing others through questioning motives, inflammatory language, and personal attacks undermines the ability to communicate effectively towards resolution.

## Tell and Show

All states require their lawyers to adhere to ethical rules modeled after the Model Rules of Professional Conduct promulgated by the ABA but also to state specific aspirations of conduct that go by various names:

| | |
|---|---|
| Arizona: A Lawyer's Creed of Professionalism | Arkansas: Code of Professional Courtesy |
| California: Various County bar associations | Georgia: Lawyer's Creed and Aspirational Statement on Professionalism |
| Colorado: Principles of Professionalism | Hawai'i: Guidelines for Professional Courtesy and Civility |
| Connecticut: Lawyer's Principles of Professionalism | Idaho: Standards for Civility in Professional Conduct |
| Delaware: Principles of Professionalism for Delaware Lawyers | Iowa: Standards for Professional Conduct |
| District of Columbia: Voluntary Standards for Civility in Professional Conduct | Kansas: Pillars of Professionalism |
| Florida: Guidelines for Professional Condict | Kentucky: Code of Professional Courtesy |
| Louisiana Code of Professionalism | Montana: Standards of Professional Courtesy to Clients and Among Attorneys |
| Maryland: Code of Civility | New Hampshire: Professionalism Creed |
| Massachusetts: Statement on Lawyer Professionalism | New Jersey: Principles of Professionalism |
| Minnesota: Professionalism Aspirations | New Mexico: Creed of Professionalism |

| | |
|---|---|
| Mississippi: Lawyer's Creed | New York: Statements of Client's Rights and Responsibilities; Standards of Civility |
| Missouri: Tenets for Professional Courtesy | North Carolina: Professional Creed |
| Ohio: A Lawyer's Creed, A Lawyer's Aspirational Ideals | Utah: Standards of Professionalism and Civility |
| Oklahoma: Standards of Professionalism | Vermont: Principles of Professional Conduct |
| Oregon: Statement of Professionalism | Virginia: Principles of Professionalism for Virginia Lawyers |
| Pennsylvania: Code of Civility | Washington: Code of Professionalism |
| South Carolina: Standards of Professionalism and Statement of Principles | West Virginia: Standards of Professional Conduct |
| Texas: The Texas Lawyer's Creed: A Mandate for Professionalism | Wisconsin: Standard of Courtesy and Decorum for the Courts of Wisconsin |

These codes and standards establish a baseline of professional conduct. Harsh tones invite a similar response from the party opposite which, in turn, creates an escalating spiral of hostility that makes resolution more difficult. And, candidly, focusing on demonizing clouds focus on the actual legal issues and evidence, and distracts from the merits and ultimate resolution.

*Lesson: Hatred is no a substitute for a strategy. Listen to military strategist Sun Tzu from 600 B.C.:" If you know the enemy and yourself you need not fear the results of a hundred battles." You need to see the opposition clearly and assess them accurately."*

## Tool No. 2: Picking up the Phone

Old school? Yes, but effective in reaching resolution. Call the lawyer opposite to introduce yourself, or to say hello if you know them from a previous matter, "I see we are on opposing sides of a new matter. Look forward to working with you again." This type of communication comes with several advantages:

### Tell and Show

Advances to calling the lawyer opposite:

- **Speed and Convenience**

A quick way to initiate contact, gauge potential settlement interest, and possibly expedite early resolution discussions.

- **Building Rapport**

Rapport does not mean that you charm your way into another's good graces, or that the road to resolution will be smooth and without bumps. But it does mean that a professional connection is made which is useful in subsequent communications.

- **Information Gathering**

Ask one question in all communication actions: Am I better off for having done it? Here, a call can start to enlighten you on the party opposite's needs, priorities, and feelings.

*Lesson: Old school works!*

#### FINDING YOUR VOICE

Make a list of topics to broach with a lawyer opposite, that have nothing to do with your matter. The topics should not be wildly intrusive. Nor should they be so neutral as to have little chance of building a rapport that leads to comfortable and professional interactions. Examples might be the demands of the workday, upcoming vacations, the scramble to gets kids ready for school, a hobby or pastime for either of you. Professor LeBoeuf likes to ask general questions about law practice. How do you manage overlapping vacations in your office? Or what timekeeping/

bookkeeping/case management program do you like best? Everybody likes to offer advice, so let them.

Consider a difficult conversation that you need to have. It can be with anybody, so long as your initial impulse was to send a text or email. Now plan a telephone call instead. Draft an outline or checklist of what you would like to address. Start with ways to center and acknowledge the person you will call. Even a simple question such as, "how is your day going" can open a dialogue that humanizes and relaxes the listener (and you). Consider how you will phrase what needs to be said. Prepare yourself to listen to what is said to you. Outline the responses you expect, and how you will respond. Often a fair and reasonable response—that defuses emotion—is to neutrally acknowledge that you have heard the points expressed, will consider the matter, and will resume the conversation later.

## Tool No. 3: Breaking Bread

The phrase "breaking bread" is Biblical in origin. It is now engrafted onto the legal system, referring to lawyers socializing with one another outside of formal proceedings. If appropriate, a lawyer should consider sharing a meal with counsel opposite. The American Inns of Court brings lawyers together as a group to do just that; consider doing so one on one with counsel opposite.

### Tell and Show

Professional Boundaries: It's important to differentiate between professional courtesy and allowing personal relationships to compromise a lawyer's duty of zealous advocacy for their client. Lawyers must remain objective and prioritize their client's interests, even when interacting with opposing counsel.

Ethical Obligations: While engaging in personal interactions can be beneficial, lawyers must always adhere to ethical rules, such as Model Rule 4.2 (Communication with Person Represented by Counsel), which prohibits direct communication with a represented party without their lawyer's consent.

As you can see, engaging in personal interactions with opposing counsel, though sometimes viewed with suspicion, can offer several benefits for lawyers and their clients.

➢ **Improved Communication and Cooperation**

Building rapport and trust through personal interactions can facilitate open communication and make it easier to discuss case-related matters, explore settlement options, and resolve disputes efficiently.

When lawyers have a positive relationship, they are more likely to engage in frank discussions rather than resorting to tactical posturing, which can lead to faster and less expensive resolutions for clients.

➢ **Reduced Stress and Increased Civility**

The legal profession can be highly stressful and fostering a positive and cooperative atmosphere through civil interactions can contribute to stress reduction for all involved.

Civility and courtesy between opposing counsel can prevent disputes from escalating unnecessarily and avoid "scorched earth" tactics that rarely benefit clients.

Maintaining civility aligns with ethical standards of the legal profession, reducing the likelihood of ethical dilemmas or disciplinary actions.

➢ **Enhanced Reputation and Client Satisfaction**

Lawyers who consistently demonstrate civility and professionalism earn a reputation for integrity and trustworthiness, which can lead to increased client trust and referrals.

Open and effective communication fostered by positive relationships with opposing counsel can lead to better outcomes for clients, thereby enhancing client satisfaction.

### ➢ More Efficient Case Management

Personal interactions can help lawyers assess the other side's motivations, strengths, and weaknesses, which can be valuable in developing negotiation strategies and trial tactics.

By understanding the opposing counsel's perspective, lawyers can better advise their clients and navigate the legal process more effectively.

### ➢ Considerations

Transparency and Client Consent: If a lawyer has a close personal relationship (e.g., friendship, intimate involvement) with opposing counsel, they may need to disclose this to their client and obtain informed consent to continue with the representation.

***By Way of Illustration:***

Early in her career, Professor LeBoeuf had such ongoing conflict on one of her cases with counsel opposite, that the judge at the end of yet another contentious hearing ordered both lawyers to go to lunch or dinner with one another. Judge gave further instruction that counsel was to talk about anything but the case. Resisting the urge to say, "Fine, if she pays," Professor LeBoeuf thanked the judge, and soon found herself sitting at lunch with "the enemy." It became surprisingly clear that there were plenty of things to talk about, and they had nothing to do with the case. As each lawyer listened to the other talk about their personal lives, interests, and families, they each managed to rehumanize the other. Back on track, the two counsel were able to reduce their interpersonal conflict and better serve their clients. To this day, Professor LeBoeuf remembers that sometimes the best way to advance a case is to call the other counsel and talk about anything but the case.

***By Way of Illustration:***

At the start of his legal career, Professor Maslanka prosecuted unfair labor practice cases on behalf of the National Labor Relations Board. He was assigned one in East Texas. Counsel opposite was in his 70s and local legend as a lawyer. At the lunch break on first day of trial, counsel opposite ambled towards him and said "Let's go to lunch. The hospital cafeteria is the only place to eat in this town." Whereupon Professor Maslanka reared up and said "Well, I am a lawyer for the United States government, and it would look highly improper for me to go to lunch with opposing counsel." The lawyer then, with a both pity and annoyance replied, "Son, I have been in cases over the last fifty years a lot more important than this p***s ant one and not a one of my opposing lawyers ever refused to go to lunch with me." Professor Maslanka reports that the Salisbury steak in the cafeteria was actually pretty good.

*Lesson: Effective communication flourishes in the right environment.*

## Tool No. 4: Send a "Demand" Letter

This is an unfortunate label. It's unfortunate because overly aggressive labels drive overly contentious content. The result is a "demand" letter placing a premium on cajoling, threatening, intimidating. How do people—how do you—react when on the receiving end of such a communication? Consider that many demand letters are sent out of the blue and by lawyers who do not know the party opposite or the counsel opposite. The result is not a road to resolution but rather battle lines drawn early, positions hardened at the outset, accusations flung back and forth. As Italian diplomat Niccolo Machiavelli observed, "wars begin when you will, but they do not end when you please." You and your client decide at the outset how it will be.

So, reframe the "demand" mindset into an "education" mindset. Consider a tone that there is now an opportunity for the recipient to resolve the issue in everyone's best interests. Offer a collaborative process, not a combative one.

### Tell and Show

If the goal is resolution, then it is a factually based communication clothed in conciliatory language. Consider this opening paragraph to a letter seeking peaceful resolution, not unlimited war:

***By Way of Illustration:***

Dear ________,

I represent _____ in connection with this notice to you of your breach of contractual obligations and tortious interference with ______ business relationships.

I want to start by telling you that they directed me to convey to you that it would like to reach a resolution with you on an amicable basis, and we invite you to engage in a discussion for that purpose.

Having said that, I must also set forth some facts and law in order to better inform you of the nature of the dispute and to satisfy legal requirements.

[insert facts and law here]

Of course, I have not heard what you have to say so I welcome you to contact me to explain if I have recited any of the facts incorrectly. I also want you to know that ________ is not bent on keeping you from working in a non-competitive position in ___ or anywhere else. You could even apply what you learned about the ___ industry working for ______ in _______. _______ only seeks to enforce the contract.

*Lesson: How you say something is just as important as what you say.*

## Tool No. 5: Lay the Groundwork for Resolution in Discovery

Discovery and resolution are not two separate threads. Rather they are twisted together like a pretzel. Set the tone as you proceed with the case.

### Tell and Show

How should you end the deposition of the party opposite? Yes, they can be contentious. But you will see the party opposite later, either at an informal settlement conference or in formal mediation. Leaving a positive impression is important in future negotiations. *If true,* think about this as a close:

***By Way of Illustration:***

*Lawyer:* Ms. Party Opposite, did I give you a chance to say everything that you wanted to say in this deposition?

*Party Opposite:* Yes (or if "no" let the Party Opposite say what they want).

*Lawyer:* I know giving a deposition can be a challenging experience. And I want to thank you for your professionalism and courtesy.

There is no downside.

*Lesson: Always be resolving.*

## II. RESOLUTION THROUGH MEDIATION

Mediation is a more formalized type of settlement discussion. The parties meet with a neutral mediator, usually a lawyer, who seeks to mediate or broker a resolution of the dispute. Communication is threefold: the lawyer to counsel opposite; the lawyer to the mediator; the lawyer to the client. These communications occur before mediation, during mediation, and after mediation.

### The Challenge: What Must You Do Before Mediation?

Communication is directed both outward and inward. Outward to the mediator and the party opposite; inward to the client. Yes, just like a juggler with three balls.

### Tool No. 1: Pick the Mediator with the Right Communication Style

In practice, you might get a question on who is the "best" mediator. Wrong question. The right question is who is the right mediator for *this* case. As we will see, mediator communication styles should be in sync with your client's communication style.

#### Tell and Show

Drill down further and assess whether it is your client or the party opposite that needs the most convincing to settle. Let's go back to communication styles. Does your client need a soft-spoken approach or a direct one? One based on analytical facts or on subjective feelings? Same for the party opposite.

For communication styles, there is a special overlay for mediators as described by Texas based mediator Will Pryor. He teaches us that a key communication issue for mediation is whether the mediator uses an "evaluative" or "non-evaluative" style. The latter means that the mediator never expresses an opinion on which party has the stronger case; the former means that the mediator does form an opinion and is not shy about sharing it. Pryor writes:

> I am a champion of evaluative mediation. I have opinions. I express them. My experience, credibility, and reputation, as well as my ability to evaluate cases, is why people come to see me. Mediators should not, in my view, argue with one side that their case is terrible and their prospects poor, and then argue the opposite view with their adversary. *"A Short and Happy Guide to Mediation"* (West Academic 2014).

There are contrary views. For the lawyer, consider always—first and foremost—the communication needs of your client. A final and important point. Getting to resolution is not the goal of mediation; rather it is getting to a resolution that your client finds preferrable to proceeding with the case whether they are signing the settlement check or receiving it. The mediator is a crucial component of that goal.

*Lesson: There is a Texas expression, "The only things in the middle of the road are yellow stripes and dead armadillos." Keep that in mind when picking a mediator.*

## Tool No. 2: "Explain" Mediation to Your Client

Here, we again embrace a fulsome definition of "explain" as "to make an idea or situation clear to some by describing it in detail or by revealing relevant facts or details." This entails more than "just the facts" as in a police procedural.

## Tell and Show

Here are the basic facts that the client must understand:

- The party opposite and their lawyer will be present.
- The mediation will be at the offices of the mediator Why? It is a neutral location as opposed to the office of one of the lawyers?
- The parties will be in separate rooms as the mediator shuttles back and forth between them, trying to arrive at a resolution.
- There might be a joint session where both parties are present. They come in two flavors: one in which each side gets to represent its case to the others (uncommon) and one in which only the mediator speaks, setting out the rules of the mediation. This will be decided before the mediation.
- The mediation will likely last all day so plan on being there the entire day and perhaps even into the evening (except when a half-day is agreed upon).
- There is likely to be lots of down time. Be prepared to hear offers that you believe are absurd. Patience is key.
- Explain that no one wants to be seen as giving up more than they get. Because of this natural human tendency, mediation is usually a *process*.
- If agreement is reached on the settlement terms, then a settlement document will be signed by you at the end of the mediation and is binding on you. No buyer's remorse.

But this is only the surface. You also need to communicate the dynamics of a mediation to the client.

***By Way of Illustration:***

Here is the story beneath the surface: Clients will ask you a lot about how they are supposed to relate with the party opposite. While this might be your hundredth mediation, never forget that it is likely their first. And always keep in mind that the client is in a position of conflict with the party opposite translating often into emotional reactions, a flight or fight response, and even physical manifestations. First, before talking to the client about mediation strategies and goals, determine if you need to address these concerns after going over the surface mechanics:

> *Lawyer:* Malik, now that we've gone over the basics, and before we get into strategies for the mediation, I want to talk to you about any concerns you might have about the mediation. Sometimes, clients are concerned about whether they need to shake the hand of the person suing them. That is 100% up to you. Our goal is to get a resolution that you are satisfied with, and a handshake can be a good place to start, but if you are too uncomfortable don't worry about it. Sally (person suing) is likely wondering the same thing.
>
> Now, up to this point a lot of case decisions have been made on my end—discovery strategies, dealing with counsel opposite, scheduling depositions. (Pause).
>
> Mediation changes all that. At the mediation, the mediator may address you directly. While I will be at your side, decisions on settlement and the future of this lawsuit will be up to you. So, I want to talk about that dynamic now so that it does not come as a surprise to you. And to let you know that the focus is now on you and that the decision is yours.

Now at this point many lawyers ask, "do you have any questions?" As my mother taught me "the more something goes without saying the more it needs it to be said." (Or say: "This might all be a bit confusing to you because you've never been to mediation. Now is the time to ask.")

*Lesson: It only takes an extra few minutes to ensure clarity. Take them.*

## Tool No. 3: "Explain" the Role of the Mediator to Your Client

The mediator is usually an unfamiliar concept to the client. So, a detailed explanation is best used.

*Ineffective:* "The mediator is a neutral who is here only to broker a settlement, not to take sides."

*Effective:* "The mediator is not the decisionmaker. You are."

***By Way of Illustration:***

Try telling this to the client:

*Lawyer*: "A mediator is unlike any other person you have met. Their role is not as a trusted friend or an adversary. Nor is their role as a decision maker or a complete neutral.

Rather the mediator is there to help the parties arrive at a solution that works for them. You should understand that the mediator may develop a preference or liking for one side's case over the others. Mediators often keep their own report cards grading themselves by how many cases they settle. They believe it is good public relations for them. So do not be surprised if they seem to like one side better than the other, as they push the Parties towards resolution.

But always keep in mind that they do not make decisions nor can they force you to; and the judge will only learn from the mediator whether you settled or did not settle—nothing more. I know this is a lot to take in. So, if you have any questions that is understandable. And now is a good time to ask."

*Lesson: This explanation tells the client that mediation is a dynamic, not a static, experience for them!*

## Tool No. 4: "Explain" Your Insights to Your Mediator

There is no ethical prohibition on pre-mediation *ex parte* contact with a mediator. Communication can take the form of a formal mediation settlement, with or without exhibits, or even a phone call. And, as an additional incentive, when you tell the mediator not to repeat certain information to the other side, that information is confidential absent your client's consent. Ethical persuasion can extend beyond a bloodless statement. Your client deserves it, and a mediator is grateful for it.

## Tell and Show

Back to Mediator Pryor, who writes:

> A better practice than just a written submission is to take full advantage of the confidentiality cloak, and to call the mediator or schedule a telephone conference. In such a conversation, either the day before or perhaps a week prior to the mediation, you and the mediator can discuss any aspect of the case, and perhaps share topics best not put in writing. . . A negotiation dance, like a budding romance, can begin with very subtle overtures. A twenty or thirty-minute conversation, unlike a written submission, is not a communication of what you think the mediator *should* know, it includes those issues that the mediator *wants* (to know).

***By Way of Illustration:***

Here is a checklist of possible topics to discuss with the mediator prior to the mediation:

- ☑ Clients with unrealistic expectations of mediation
- ☑ Clients—or the party opposite—with a difficult personality or challenging communication style. Draw upon your knowledge of the Birkman types discussed in Section II
- ☑ Your relationship and history (if any) with counsel opposite
- ☑ Your "splash zone" of settlement—that is, the range of dollars you are looking for. Ethical note: this will anchor the mediator who will work towards your zone but only use an actual zone agreed upon beforehand with your client. Honesty with the mediator, not manipulation

☑ Prior settlement demands and/or negotiations.

*Lesson: A famous movie uses the phrase, "Always be selling." Modify it here to "Always be negotiating."*

## Tool No. 5: Define "Success" with Your Client

All effective communication depends on a shared language. Without a shared language, we engage in an illusion of communication. If a mediation is to be successful, the lawyer and the client must agree on what they see as its endpoint.

### Tell and Show

To define with your client, ask the right questions:

- When we formed the ACR, your objectives were ABC. Is that still the case? Under MR 1.2 the client sets the objectives of the representation, but it need not and often does not remain fixed.
- If different, how has it changed?
- Why has it changed?
- What would you like to be able to say after the mediation is concluded?

Note that objectives can change for a variety of reasons. Discovery might reveal that the client's case is weaker or stronger than initially believed. Changed circumstances can shift the focus from winning on liability to minimizing damages or from maximizing damages to avoiding a loss on liability. Or the client's desire to take a principled stand might fade as time goes by (and as legal fees pile up!). Pre-mediation, your communication goal as a lawyer is gauging whether client objectives have changed. If so, empower the client to embrace this change.

***By Way of Illustration:***

Professor Maslanka represented an aircraft manufacturer in a case under the Americans with Disabilities Act. The plaintiff was not hired because his client believed that he lacked the motor skills for the often fine manufacturing tasks required in aircraft assembly. The plaintiff had suffered a head injury several years earlier. At an early-stage mediation, the plaintiff's lawyer demanded a seven-figure settlement, announcing that she would not budge from the demand. The mediation was unsuccessful.

Later, during his deposition, arguably due to his head injury, plaintiff showed a marked decline in cognitive and motor skills. The mediation after the deposition was successful, when the plaintiff dropped his demand considerably.

*Lesson: Embrace fluidity.*

## Tool No. 6: Listen to the Client

Always be attuned to what the client is saying. While you are the expert in the law, they are the expert in their business.

***By Way of Illustration:***

Professor LeBoeuf handled a case for a client who built modular structures for business use. Their customer, a nonprofit providing pre-school programs to economically disadvantaged children, had ordered a modular building for school use. To everyone's horror (not least Professor LeBoeuf's, imagining the jury argument), the building developed mold and the children had to be educated at a temporary site elsewhere. There were many parties involved, with many competing theories, supported by everybody's respective experts—the soil was improperly tested and held too much water; the land was improperly graded and water drained to a point under the building; the building was improperly built or installed; and so on. The client's in-house counsel, who excelled at negotiation, wanted an early mediation.

Professor LeBoeuf reluctantly agreed, thinking the parties were too entrenched and the facts too unclear. Then the client proposed holding the mediation at the home office of the non-profit. What?! And while traveling to the mediation, the client insisted on stopping to buy pastries for everybody. Once there, let everybody else speak first.

Professor LeBoeuf and her client learned that the nonprofit was going to lose their federal funding if the matter was not resolved quickly—a circumstance that would have greatly multiplied the damages, and one they would not have discovered through normal discovery until after the fact. The case resolved, not least due to the courtesy and kindness of the client, who knew to first feed everyone, and then to listen quietly. But this was only could take place because the ACR was a healthy one from creation forward. A strong ACR produces effective communication between the lawyer and her client.

*Lesson: When in doubt, go to the source—the client.*

## The Challenge: What Do I Say at the Mediation?

Let's use a checklist. Mediator is briefed. Check. Goals are confirmed or changed. Check. Notebooks for you, clients and mediator are assembled and packed. Check. Now, figure out what you will say at the mediation.

## Tool No. 1: Communicate a Conciliatory Tone, if Warranted

A mediation starts with either a joint substantive session or only a meet-and-greet session. If the first then you, your client and the lawyer and client opposite meet in a conference room with the mediator, state your respective positions, and then move off to your own rooms, with the mediator shuttling back and forth between rooms.

Consider a conciliatory tone in a joint session, while also firmly stating facts and legal theories. An aggressive tone tends to set the mediation two steps backward as opposed to one step forward. You can always escalate from a moderate stance but can seldom de-escalate from an extreme one.

### Tell and Show

Your manner is a form of communication. So, when giving your presentation in a joint session, look directly at the party opposite, not the lawyer opposite. After all, the party opposite is the decision maker. Your tone as well is a form of communication. A moderate one demonstrating empathy to the party opposite while still standing firm on your client's position is a form of communication.

***By Way of Illustration:***

> Ms. Jones, we met before at your deposition. My client and I are glad to see you again. We promise that we are here today in good faith to try and resolve this matter on a principled basis. But, if we cannot, we also promise that we are ready to go the distance and take this case to trial. But regardless of the route that is taken, we also promise that we will not—in this mediation or in a trial—question your motives in this lawsuit. We know that in your heart you believe that a wrong was done to you. But we do not see it that way. We will listen to what you have to say and all we ask now is that you will listen to what we have to say.

This communications approach defuses anger, fosters conciliation, leads to reconciliation. A caveat: if the party opposite committed a bad act, for which your client seeks to hold them accountable, then say so. Directness is also part of the tool belt.

*Lesson: "Give peace a chance." John Lennon and Yoko Ono.*

## Tool No. 2: Use the Language of Brackets

Every legal proceeding contains its own particular lingo. For mediation, an illustration is "brackets." Use of brackets is a common technique of mediators when they get stuck in shuttle diplomacy.

***By Way of Illustration:***

Los Angeles mediator Denise Madigan explains the process in her insightful article, "Bracketing 101" (Advocate, August 2017). Let's say that party A demands $1,000,000 to settle; Party Z counters with $25,000. The word glacial pace comes to mind with further offers /counteroffers consisting of minimal increments. Madigan explains how to avoid being stuck in park:

> With impasse looming, a mediator (or party) will look for ways to "interrupt" the process and restart negotiations at numbers much closer to one another. Bracketing can do just that by enabling each party to make a large move while reducing its risk of exposure.

So, a bracket can be proposed of ($750,000/$500,000), meaning Party A will lower their demand to $750,000 if Party B increased their offer to $500,000. This is safer for Party A than simply dropping to $750,000 as a demand and hoping for a good response. What is ultimately communicated (ideally) is the midpoint at which the parties can settle (here, $625,000).

Madigan notes that, like any form of communication, there can be misunderstandings. At times, the bracket midpoint does not signal the intended midpoint; at other times, if both parties have accepted the mediator's bracket, there can be confusion about which party makes the next move. As with all communications, there is no substitute for anticipating possible miscommunications and planning for them.

*Lesson: Brackets can be especially effective if you tell the mediator your "splash zone."*

## Tool No. 3: Consider Saying "No"

Conventional wisdom: failing to settle at mediation is unethical and unprofessional. The reality: saying no to a settlement is a tool on your toolbelt.

### Tell and Show

Two scenarios in which "no" works.

*Scenario No. 1:* The one with the better case gets to say "no"

The opposing sides to litigation are never equally matched on the facts. Yes, one party might out-work the party opposite, or be able to deploy greater resources, or play a badly dealt hand more skillfully. But also, one side typically enjoys an advantage on the facts. So, if a client and their lawyer who enjoy a fact advantage prefer to insist on their desired resolution, they should do so, knowing there is always a risk when the case is put into the hands of a jury of strangers.

*Scenario No. 2:* Trying to squeeze out the last dollar

When you've been in mediation all day, a strange phenomenon occurs. We call it the "Gravitational Pull of Settlement", often caused by using Tool No. 2. A party concludes—often unconsciously—that the case will settle. In fact, the party is already starting to spend the settlement money in their heads (or saved litigation costs). This is not unlike a satellite orbiting the earth, yanked in by gravity. It's just a matter of time before the satellite collides with earth.

It goes like this:

*Lawyer/Client:* Our final offer is $50,000 with the following terms included in the settlement agreement: (insert)

*Mediator:* I will tell the other side and be right back.

(15 minutes go by and the mediator returns.)

*Mediator:* Well, good news! We have a deal if you pick up their portion of the mediator's fee.

*Lawyer/Client:* Well, we said final offer so the answer is no, we will not.

Almost invariably, the party opposite caves.

*Lesson: "No" is a full sentence.*

## Tool No. 4: The Client Makes Decisions, Not the Lawyer

From time to time, clients try put us in the position of making settlement decisions for them. Model Rule 1.2 tells us that clients make such ultimate decisions. And while citing them to the substance of MR 1.2 is communication, it is hardly effective communication. So, what do we say?

### Tell and Show

The reasons for the question are varied. But regardless of the motivation, there are several communication tools to use before answering the question: "What would you do?" First, the tools:

- Prior to a mediation or in the early stages of litigation, focus the client's attention on what she has done to resolve the matter. By way of example, ask straightforward questions on what the client perceives to be options; "What have you already done to try and resolve the matter?" or "what options have you thought about trying or are thinking about trying?"

- Focus the client on their objectives in the matter. Is the objective to try the lawsuit because (generally with a corporate client) a settlement would only encourage others to sue or is the objective to manage risk by settling? Always—when focus is being lost—ask "What are we are we trying to achieve?"

  When Professor Maslanka was in practice, a client he was representing in a wrongful termination case, asked very directly: "What is your philosophy on settling a case?" She was a hard charger, a Red in the Birkman universe (Chapter II) and was expecting a direct answer. Professor Maslanka gave her one: "Does this case go to a value your company holds dear? If so, then consider fighting. If not, then it is more likely a purely business decision, so consider settlement."

Now to answering directly the question of "what would you do?" It is acceptable to tell the client what you think as long as the dividing line is made clear, such as:

- "I will take my lawyer hat off for a moment and put on my client hat. . ."
- "If I were sitting in the CEO chair and it was my company to run, then I would . . ."

After this answer, however, the lawyer should refocus the client on all the options presenting themselves, not simply the one the lawyer would pick if he or she were in the driver's seat.

Barriers: know them and respect them.

***By Way of Illustration:***

Professor LeBoeuf represented clients in probate court, daughters of a man swept into guardianship by non-family members, then stripped of his assets by a team of professionals claiming to make decisions in his "best interest". Before he died, their father was isolated from his family, and the family wasn't informed of his death until after the funeral. The daughters, appalled at their father's treatment and the loss of his legacy, and grieving what they too had lost, obtained all the relief they could from the courts, but it was incomplete. Their only remaining avenue was to appeal the points on which they had lost. Financially and emotionally exhausted, they asked, "What would you do, if your father had been treated so cruelly?"

Here you must lean heavily into the "counselor" part of your legal role. In such a case, clients need more than your handicapping of their odds, or your direction regarding the next best legal step. Listening deeply, it is important to hear the question implicit in "What would you do?" Sometimes, as attorney and counselor, you may discern a different question—"Have we done enough?" or "Is it okay to settle/stop fighting/non-suit or dismiss", as the case may be. What clients often need from their counsel is the 30,000-foot view that you bring, as a professional, with your understanding of legal options, potential outcomes, and also the emotions wrapped up in the case by the litigants.

A proper response may take the form of assurances that clients have honored (in this case) their father with their actions and made a record of the harm done. It may take the form of advice that clients have taken the case as far as it can reasonably go with any good result. There will be times in your cases when the best advice is to lay down the sword and stop putting good money after bad.

Helping clients to frame their victories (which are not always a complete and total win), understand what is realistic, and recognize the limits of the law, are key parts of serving as counsel. Honesty, transparency, and seeing the client in their humanity and their struggle, are necessary components for doing so.

*Lesson: Know your boundaries.*

## Tool No. 5: Communicate Clearly on Settlement Terms

This is a two-way street: the lawyer to the client, then the lawyer to counsel opposite. The failure to be clear in either direction results in failed mediation.

## Tell and Show

Never fear looking clueless. Ever. When you hear “usual terms” or “the standard agreement” your ears must perk up, with questions triggered as to the details. Here is a checklist for your client.

### *Settlement Language Checklist*

- ☑ Do we want a non-disparagement clause, with or without a penalty for breach? (Note: a non-disparagement clause is a contractual provision that prevents one or more parties from making negative, false, or misleading statements about one another.)
- ☑ Do we want a confidentiality clause, with or without a penalty for breach? If so, can the meditation terms still be with immediate family members, accountants, and/or lawyers?
- ☑ Will there be a payout over time of the settlement amount and is there a penalty for missing a payment?
- ☑ Will interest accrue?
- ☑ Any contingencies that are important to the client, such as a letter of apology or return of a work computer?
- ☑ How broad should the release of claims be? For example, do we give releases of only the claims in the lawsuit, or of all matters, known or unknown, through date of settlement?
- ☑ In case of a default on settlement payment, will the payment amount be accelerated (i.e. all due at once) or will there be entry of an agreed judgment?
- ☑ How will the payments be made and to whom?

*Lesson: A deal is not done until the deal is done.*

## Tool No. 6: Know There are Unethical Offers

In contentious litigation, feelings will run high against a lawyer opposite by a party opposite. But can a lawyer ethically propose or accept a settlement term relating to the lawyer opposite?

### Tell and Show

Here is Model Rule 5.6: Restrictions on the Right to Practice:

"A lawyer shall not participate in offering or making:

> [. . .] (b) an agreement in which a restriction on the lawyer's right to practice is part of the settlement of a client controversy."

***By Way of Illustration:***

During mediation of a products liability case, the Chief Financial Officer turns to her counsel and says "I hate that lawyer who is suing us! Make it so that we never see him again and he does not sue again for this so-called product defect. It's a condition of settlement." Certainly, this is a reasonable request from a businessperson schooled in capitalism, not legal ethics. But as we see from MR 5.6 (followed by most, but not all states), it is a violation of ethics to offer *or* to accept. Why? The public should be given their choice of lawyer without restrictions on their choices. And makes the lawyer's future activities a condition of settlement creates a conflict with their client.

And no end runs around the Rule. So, it is a violation to say to counsel opposite, "Gee, let's hire you as a consultant on these product liability cases at $50,000 a year. We will include that in the settlement agreement!" It is a violation for counsel opposite to agree.

*Lesson: A violation to offer, a violation to accept.*

## The Challenge: What Do I Say Post-Mediation?

Your practice thrives through your reputation as a lawyer. So, post-mediation opportunities for communication should be considered.

## Tool No. 1: Send an After-Action Report to the Client

Nothing says "I care" to a client as much as sending (at no cost) an After-Action Report to the client post-mediation. Lawyers should always aspire to leave the client better off post-ACR then when the ACR is formed.

### Tell and Show

This is a practice borrowed from the military. After every engagement—win, lose, draw—commanders write a report describing what went right and how to replicate, and what went wrong and how to avoid. Blame is not assessed; fingers are not pointed. The goal is incremental improvement.

***By Way of Illustration:***

**To: Corporate Client**

**From: Lawyer**

**Re: After Action Report Post Settlement on Wrongful Termination Lawsuit**

Juan, it was a privilege to represent you in litigation, I am pleased we were able to resolve this lawsuit at mediation. As promised, here is an After-Action Report setting out what we learned from the litigation and some suggestions for improvement:

- Factual Summary

  [Insert Your Facts Here.]

- Lessons Learned

*Lesson No 1:* No multiple levels of review of the termination

Recall that the plaintiff's lawyer accused the company of lacking due process before terminating the plaintiff. My experience with juries, and what I hear from jury consultants, is that jurors will look to see if there were several sets of eyes on the decision to take away an employee's job. If so, that is a positive for you in jury trial.

Suggestion: Develop a multilevel process which is strictly followed, including always looping in human resources.

*Lesson No. 2:* Immediate termination as opposed to suspension to allow investigation

Another line of attack against the company was that there was an immediate termination as opposed to an investigation to determine the facts prior to any discipline being imposed.

Suggestion: Place employee on unpaid or paid leave (depending on the circumstances) while an investigation is conducted. This is important because the law takes a snapshot of what you knew about the employee's misconduct at the time of the termination. You therefore would be limited to testifying about what you knew at the time you made the decision.

I hope this helps. Let us know if we can be of service to you and your organization.

Regards,
Lawyer

*Lesson: Always leave the client better off than when you found them.*

## Tool No. 2: Thank Counsel Opposite for Their Professionalism

Where will your business come from? Referrals from other lawyers, especially those whom you litigated against. They know you in action, the depth of your knowledge, the nature of your abilities.

### Tell and Show

Naturally, express such a sentiment only if true. A brief email or letter will do the trick, especially when wrapping up a mediated settlement such as when exchanging signed settlement documents.

***By Way of Illustration:***

Professor Maslanka represented companies in unlawful discrimination cases. He settled a matter with a lawyer who represented employees in such matters. An example of an email he sent:

> "Libby, just a quick note to say thanks for your courtesy and professionalism in resolving our case. If you have a referral for a company needing representation in an employment matter, I hope you will think of me. And I certainly will think of you should an individual come my way.
>
> If you happen to be downtown, let me know and we can grab lunch."

*Lesson: Develop a reputation for professionalism. It's good business.*

## Tool No. 3: Express Gratitude to the Mediator

Whether practicing in a large metro area or in a rural community there is a constant: you will be or are part of a closed-in ecosystem.

### Tell and Show

In their mediation practice, mediators meet more lawyers in a week than you might meet in a month. Regardless of whether there is a mediated settlement, thank them for their efforts.

The Harvard Business Review suggests that in a business context, such as employing a mediator, make the thank you specific, sincere and timely.

- **Be Specific**

Rather than a generic "thanks", point out any specific action or contribution they made towards resolution or attempted resolution. The first is amorphous sentiment quickly forgotten, while the second is a concrete one long remembered.

➢ **Explain the Impact**

Describe how their action or contribution drove the parties towards a settlement. Or how you appreciated the way in which the mediator dealt with your client, and seek to tie it back to any pre-mediation conversations with the mediator.

➢ **Don't Overdo It**

This is business communication, not a love letter, so make the content, and the tone, proportionate to the efforts extended.

*Lesson: These lessons come from, "Giving Thanks at Work: An HBR Guide" by Amy Gallo, November 24, 202. Give it a read. Saying "Thanks" costs nothing.*

## III. RESOLUTION THROUGH ADJUDICATION

Sooner or later, whatever your area of practice, you'll be involved—directly or indirectly—in a trial or a binding arbitration. It is inevitable. Knowing communication fundamentals in opening statements and closing arguments is a decided advantage when the time comes.

### A. Opening Statements

**The Challenge: How Do You Write an Effective Opening Statement?**

Consider a blank yellow legal tablet or blue rays emanating from your computer screen. You might ask yourself where in the world do I start filling in the void. We don't want to go all Zen on you, but you start at the start.

**Tool No. 1: Use Model Jury Charges to Develop the Case Theme**

The opening starts with reviewing the Complaint and the Answer/Affirmative Defenses to draft the charge. Model jury charges are published by courts and bar associations. They set out what a jury will be told as to the law and the questions they will be required to answer in rendering a verdict. While all people are created equal, all facts are not. The facts you develop—and what you therefore say in opening—must be filtered through the applicable law. This is the *legal* theory of your case.

## Tool No. 2: Create a Case Frame for Opening Statement

The case frame is the focal point of your opening. While some lawyers refer to a "case theory," we use frame because it is more specific and descriptive of what is taking place, namely, how the case facts are filtered through a jury's shared understanding of the world. It must be clear, simple and memorable. And most importantly, it must resonate with a pre-existing belief of the decision maker.

### Tell and Show

> *Myth:* Jurors make up their minds after hearing all the evidence at trial.
>
> *Reality:* Jurors make up their minds, in large part, before ever stepping into the courtroom.

Each of us walks around with baked in beliefs from living our lives. Cognitive theory supports this view. Here is a study conducted at Emory University. During a run-up to an election researchers took thirty voters—50% strong Republicans, 50% strong Democrats. Each group was shown videos of their respective candidates clearly contradicting themselves on various positions. As expected, each group saw no contradictions in their candidates though they readily saw the contradictions in the candidates opposite.

Now to the unexpected. Brain scans were taken of subjects in both groups during the playing of both videos. The part of the brain associated with reasoning—to be specific, the dorsolateral prefrontal cortex—was quiet as a church mouse when the video of the candidate opposite was played. But the part of the ventral striatum—associated with rewards—was lighting up like a pin ball machine when their candidates were speaking. The conclusion: the brain is rewarded for confirming what it already believes, that is, pre-existing beliefs, and not rewarded by what the brain does not already believe. Persuasive communication therefore depends on rewarding the brain by finding a frame most in sync with your argument.

***By Way of Illustration:***

Ronald H. Clark, in a short gem of a book, *Addressing the Jury: Opening Statement and Closing Argument* gives a list of frames to which we have added a few, along with a suggestion on how to use them. Expounding these frames can be the first words you say in an opening:

*Frame No. 1:* Power and Control Over Others

"This is a case about power and control. The power and control that one person exercises over another. That Joe Smith exercised over his wife Sally. My name is Marcus Lawyer, and I represent Sally in this matter. Here is what you will learn about power and control in the next few days."

*Frame No. 2:* Accountability for One's Actions

"This is a case about being accountable for your actions. You are given a driver's license. It is a privilege. But with that privilege comes responsibility. And that privilege must be exercised wisely. My name is Letty Lawyer, and I represent Penny Client who was injured when a car driven by the defendant smashed into her car at an intersection. Here is what happened on the day of the collision."

*Frame No. 3:* Merit as a Transcendent Value

"This is a case on judging an employee for what they do at work. On their job performance. On their contributions to the company. And not on their race. My name is Kelli Lawyer, and I represent Edna Client. Let's go back to June 1 when Edna was abruptly fired from her job."

*Frame No. 4:* Fair Play as A Fundamental Virtue

"This is a case about what we learn as kids. It is about what we learn on the playground—fair play. And fair play is something that does not end in childhood but extends into the business world. My name is Quinn

Lawyer, and I represent ABC Company in this lawsuit against XYZ Company and a former employee of ABC for unfair competition. (More on this in the next Challenge.)

*Frame No. 5:* Broken Promises Are a Danger

"This is a case about a very basic rule of society, about making a promise and about keeping that promise. A case about a broken promise. My name is Orly Lawyer, and I represent Dan Jones. Dan is suing the defendant for breaking just such a promise. Here is how the promise came to be made and how it was broken."

The purpose of these frames is not only to give an overview but to plant a seed; that is, triggering a juror to start extrapolating the rest of the story. This is sometimes called "gap filling."

*Lesson: Start with a universal frame.*

## Tool No. 3: Deploying the Frame

Once a frame is settled upon, consider its delivery system. This system is the context in which you deliver the frame's message.

### Tell and Show

Here is the delivery system from the unfair competition case. The facts are that Mr. Jones left employment at *Company ABC* and went to work for a competitor, *Company XYZ,* in the same capacity as he worked at *Company ABC.* As you read the following, think about the frame that is being suggested.

Here is a possible deployment: "This is a case about what we learn as kids. It is about fair play. About what we learn on the playground. And fair play is not something that ends in childhood but extends into the business world. My name is Quinn Lawyer, and I represent ABC Company in this lawsuit against XYZ Company and ABC's former employee.

> Here is what happened. Upon being employed by ABC, Mr. Jones made an agreement with ABC not to work for a competitor and use ABC's confidential information. The case is about Mr. Jones violating that agreement. It is about *Company XYZ* hiring Mr. Jones despite knowing about this agreement. Now, let's be clear. No one from ABC is going to get on that witness stand and say, "Mr. Jones you can't leave and go to work for another company," or "*Company XYZ* you can't hire one of our employees." ABC is only saying that Mr. Jones must honor his promise—a promise he made while employed at ABC and made at a time when ABC was paying him. ABC is only saying that Company *XYZ* *must* compete fairly by not hiring Mr. Jones."

Let's deconstruct. Frames? For Jones: one's word is his bond. For Company XYZ: Fight fair and may the best company win.

*Lesson: Each a belief already held by a juror. Tap into a preexisting belief.*

## Tool No. 4: Never Start with Pointless Throat Clearing

Recall that you only have a few minutes of 100% attention by 100% of the jury. This is valuable real estate.

### Tell and Show

Do not waste valuable time with:

- Explaining that opening statement is not evidence.
- Teaching that the "the judge decides the law, and you are the judges of the facts."
- Describing an opening statement as a "roadmap."

*Lesson: If you are not stating your frame or the narrative supporting your frame, then cut the language. Period.*

## Tool No. 5: Never Start by Rebutting the Party Opposite's Frame and/or Narrative

While we will talk in a minute about dealing with bad facts in your opening, the overarching rule is *always* this: never waste time in opening by being reactive to the party opposite's frame/ narrative.

### Tell and Show

Yes, we know that it is tempting to stand up and say, "the party opposite says ABC but the truth is XYZ." Often the client will want you to do so. Don't.

While in practice, Professor Maslanka was hired to appeal an adverse jury verdict against an employer in an age discrimination lawsuit. In reading the transcript, he saw that the plaintiff's lawyer gave a blistering opening statement about the callousness of the company in firing a long time, dedicated employee. Caving into temptation, the company's lawyer listed each accusation and the company's response to each as in, "He says ABC; that is wrong, the true facts are XYZ." While no doubt satisfying, the approach backfired with the jury hearing the allegations *twice*, not once.

*Lesson: As author Steven D. Stark observes in "Writing to Win: The Legal Writer", legal briefs should be like two ships passing in the night. We agree, with one small exception to which we now turn.*

## Tool No. 6: Inoculate Against Bad Facts

Every case you will ever try deals with at least some bad facts for your client. While you cannot change the inevitable, you can manage it and—with experience and skill—flip it to your advantage.

### Tell and Show

You can ignore bad facts, or you can inoculate against them. New cognitive research supports the second approach.

Conventional cognitive theory supports the view that the party introducing a bad fact is seen by the jury as "sponsoring" that fact and the jury punishes and does not reward that sponsorship. *Robert Klonoff & Paul H. Colby, Winning Jury Trials: Trial Tactics and Sponsorship Strategy* (1990). Their advice: zip it.

But in 1993 a new study took the opposite approach. Their hypo: a man is killed in a car crash when his vehicle is overturned. The estate sues, alleging that his car was defective because it was not crash-worthy. The bad fact inserted in the scenario: the autopsy reveals that the man was drinking before the crash.

The mock jurors saw two opening statements:

No. 1: No mention of the drinking (sponsorship)

No. 2: Mention of the drinking but stating that the deceased did not have a reputation as a drinker and that the alcohol level was within the legal limit (inoculation)

Results?

- The inoculation group found the defense arguments on alcohol consumption to be less persuasive than the jurors in the sponsorship group.
- The inoculation group found the plaintiffs' lawyers to be more honest, organized, persuasive, poised and effective than the plaintiffs' lawyers who did not inoculate.
- The inoculation group had higher desire for the plaintiff to win and a lower desire for the defendant to win.

***By Way of Illustration:***

*Illustration No. 1:* Acknowledge, Then Transition

Here is one technique.

"While no one will dispute that the plaintiff had several drinks, we will dispute that the design of the car was crash-worthy."

Note the acknowledgment using a positive/negative sentence (discussed in Section II) with a quick transition to a new focus.

*Illustration No. 2:* The Power of Contrast

Music mogul Sean "Diddy" Combs was prosecuted for RICO violations, or running a criminal enterprise. Recall that he was charged with sex trafficking his girlfriend, and a video shows him beating her in a hallway. Here is part of his opening:

> "Sean Combs is a complicated man, but this is not a complicated case. This case is about love, jealousy, infidelity and money. This case is about voluntary adult choices made by capable adults in consensual relationships. The government can say repeatedly that this is not about his private sex life, but the evidence will show you that it is. Not one witness will get into this courtroom and take that witness stand and tell you that they were part of any corrupt organized criminal enterprise. And the reason is simple: There was not one. Perhaps they did not always show love to one another, the way you would with your partner, but they were in a relationship, and she was not being trafficked . . . the video shows domestic violence, not sex trafficking."
>
> *(Editorial Note: Focus how the lawyer talks about what the case is not about (more on that in a minute). The lawyer shifts into contrast between bad facts and the actual charge, which is a contrast technique we talked about at the start of this book.)*
>
> "Sean Combs has a bad temper. He sometimes gets so angry or so jealous that he is out of control. But he is not charged with being mean, he is not charged with being a jerk. He is charged for running a racketeering enterprise. We are telling you right now that he is physical, that he is a drug user. And I am telling you that he had a bit of a different sex life. Is that a federal crime? (Editorial Note: End of contrast) . . . We will not shy away from what Mr. Combs did, but we will not own the things that he did not do."

Result: a guilty verdict on the relatively minor charge of interstate transportation of women for sex and not guilty on the much more serious RICO criminal charge.

*Illustration No. 3:* Embrace the Bad Facts

The late trial lawyer Gerry Spence was defending Imelda Marcos on racketeering and fraud charges. She was the First Lady of the Philippines and accused of being part of a repressive regime. News reports stressed her country's poverty in comparison to her lavish lifestyle including closets of expensive shoes (photos of which were widely printed). Out of the box he stated:

> "She spent money. No question about that. She is a world class spender. She is a world class shopper."

But he then went on to explain that she was also a "small, fragile woman" with little grasp of "the intricacies of finance," who was manipulated by others.

Result: Not guilty.

*Lesson: As the ancient Stoics taught us, "The obstacle is the way." In other words, turn challenges into advantages.*

## Tool No. 7: Start with Your B.L.U.F.

Back to Bottom Line Up Front that we discussed in the Presentations Section. An opening statement is not a mystery novel, keeping the reader off balance, with the culprit being revealed on the last page.

### Tell and Show

The window of opportunity on the attention chart used earlier in this book comes into play here. The lawyer has only three minutes of undivided attention, So, make those three minutes count. Here are three examples of how to do so.

***By Way of Illustration:***

*No. 1:* Defense opening on a plaintiff claiming race discrimination in his termination.

> On June 1, Mr. Jones failed to perform his work responsibilities in a safe manner. His failure resulted in a pipe leak that damaged $15,000 worth of product. His failure even endangered his co-workers. Mr. Jones let down his team, his company, and most importantly himself. So, this case is about teamwork. It is about responsibility. It is about accountability.

> *(Pause)* My name is Lupe Lawyer, and I represent XYZ Company, and we look forward to now discussing these facts in more detail.

Jury consultant, Dr. Bill Kanasky Jr. of Dallas-based Courtroom Sciences writes that a B.L.U.F. approach immediately arms the jurors with your frame, giving them the "real" story. Note that this communication style uses the technique of "flashforward" going directly to the day of the termination, as opposed to a chronological order, listing all the events leading up to the termination. (like a mystery novel.) By quickly highlighting the plaintiff's role it answers the jury question of "why are we here" while simultaneously creating a sense of intrigue on the jury's part in terms of "Gee, I wonder the details of what led up to the plaintiff's failure."

*No. 2:* Defense opening on plaintiff suing for age discrimination from budgetary constraints.

> Good morning, my name is Omar Lawyer, and I represent XYZ Company. Your time is valuable, and I promise I will not waste it in this trial or in this opening. We're here today because plaintiff is no longer employed by XYZ Company. And he is disappointed in that, but disappointment is not the same thing as unlawful discrimination. Now you are likely wondering if he is not at XYZ due to his age, why is he no longer there? And the answer is very straightforward and simple. XYZ had a budget shortfall. It happens to companies. And to solve this problem, it did what companies do. It conducted a reduction-in-force, what is commonly called a RIF. And a RIF is something, as even plaintiff will acknowledge to you, that businesses do when they have a shortfall. It was never personal to the plaintiff. In this case he was included. Why? Because he was in a stand-alone position that was no longer needed.

Notice how the language seeks to normalize the idea of a RIF. This is done to divorce the decision from any unlawful motivation.

*No. 3:* Plaintiff Opening in a personal injury case

Let me take you back to August 1, 2024. It was a clear and cloudless day in XYZ city. ABC Company truck driver Ed Smith is driving down Main Street in his company truck, making deliveries. He is lost, looks down at his cell phone, checking his map app. He runs the red light at the intersection and slams into the side of my client's car. She is severely injured and is taken by ambulance to St. Luke hospital's emergency room.

Note the communication tactics used.

- The focus is always on the defendant's action, never on the plaintiff's actions. Focus always on the bad actor.
- The narrative stays in the present tense. This communication technique imparts a sense of the immediate, giving off a "you are there" feeling.
- The frame of rule breaking is presented front and center. Even the rebels among us embrace rules because they create a safe world.
- Words matter and they matter a lot. There are choices other than "slams" such as "collides" or "hits" or "crashes" but "slams" imparts a sense of noise and even violence that the other choices lack. As Mark Twain remarked, "the difference between the right word and the almost right word is the difference between a lightning bolt and a lightning bug."

Where does the "flash-forward" style come from? It is borrowed from the movies. This technique does not begin with "once upon a time." Rather it starts with the present time.

- *Goodfellas:* The brutal murder of a rival gangster
- *Casino:* An attempted robbery
- *Gangs of New York:* A violent territorial war on the streets of New York City
- *The Wolf of Wall Street:* The protagonist is shown in his prime and the movie rewinds to his earlier life

- *Kill Bill:* The start is a fight scene, and then the movie reveals a flashback for context

Why do movies do this (as well as trial lawyers)?

The viewer is primed and anticipating the answer to this question: what comes next? Back to the chart on attention span (in Section I). This approach hooks the viewer or juror in the first few minutes and maintains their attention for longer than would normally be expected.

Trial lawyer Jim M. Perdue suggests the following:

- "It started out like any other workday. . ."
- "They were the saddest words Lisa Lee ever heard: Mrs. Lee, your child is brain damaged. . ."
- "Lois, you have a tumor. We need to operate right away. . ."
- "Mary Johnson had no choice . . ."

*Lesson: Use hooks for engagement and focus.*

## Tool No. 8: Forecast What Will Not Be Coming

Opening statements are generally thought of as telling the jury about what it will hear. But effective communication is also telling the jury what it will *not* hear.

### Tell and Show

Think the way an artist thinks of "negative space" which is not just empty space but an active element contributing to the overall impact of the work of art.

***By Way of Illustration:***

This yin and yang of an opening therefore operate as complimentary pieces of an opening. Here is the yang (negative space) part of an opening after you provide your B.L.U.F.

> "You're going to hear a lot of theories about age discrimination, a lot of speculation about age discrimination in the next few days. But what you are not going to hear or see are any notes about age

discrimination, no documents supporting the claim of age discrimination, no statements from managers about age discrimination or a tendency towards discrimination. You're not, because they don't exist."

Note too that his technique comes with the bonus of undercutting the case of the party opposite. It is intended to focus the jury on asking themselves—in an anticipatory fashion: "Well, will the plaintiff come up with some documents?"

*Lesson: Communicate through omission.*

## Tool No. 9: Use Active Voice in Describing the Facts

A strong start needs to be maintained. Strong, active sentences and phrases will do that for you.

### Tell and Show

Here are some illustrations on how to do so:

- "The manager violated this rule." Declarative and thus strong as opposed to "failed to follow" which is low key and thus insipid.
- "You will learn . . ." Declarative and thus imparts certainty, authority, and a promise of further understanding. It also imparts a promise of a clear path forward by the lawyer and suggests an inevitable outcome.
- "You will hear from that witness stand . . ." Vivid and allows you to put movement into opening by using your body to point to the witness stand. Remember the body is also a communication tool.
- "You will read the language in the contract." Imparts a sense of "Yes, I am looking forward to that as opposed to 'The contract says . . .' "
- "A damages expert will show you exactly how much the losses are to the plaintiff." Again, a promise that can be looked forward to as opposed to "The plaintiff suffered ABC damages, and you will hear a damages expert explain them to you."

*Lesson: The difference between the right word/phrase and the almost right word/phrase is the difference between a lightning bolt and a lightning bug.*

## Tool No. 10: Use a Timeline

A timeline can be invaluable in opening. Professor Maslanka would sometimes use a flash-forward and then utilize a timeline in developing the facts leading to the flash-forward event. Here is how they work.

### Tell and Show

There are two types of timelines: static and interactive. A static timeline is done on a blow-up board. The downside is that it must be very simple; too many facts confuse a juror. And more importantly, jurors see the entire timeline at once and fall victim to the temptation to read ahead of where the lawyer is on the timeline.

By contrast, an interactive timeline shows events one at a time so there is no chance of a juror looking ahead. The lawyer tells a trial tech when to flash the next time segment or does it themselves.

***By Way of Illustration:***

You've been there yourself. You're watching election returns while TV hosts and their guests are rattling off statistics. What is the best path to victory for your candidate? What is the alternate path? What do early returns indicate? You're smart. You've been following the news for months. You've read article after article. But in the compressed period of the actual election, the only way you're really going to follow along is to see the graphics.

And graphics, there are lots of them Color-mapping by political party. Colored charts by county, state, and nation. Numbers and percentages kept to a minimum, or completely absent.

This is what it's like to be a juror, or an attendee at a CLE presentation. Show me.

A prevailing theory on visual learning is that information sticks better when the audience receives both image and text. Allan Paivio, of the University of Western Ontario, developed the dual-coding theory in 1971. He posited that the brain's storage of sensory information (such as images) and verbal information (such as text or spoken word) occur in separate locations, which interact and cross-reference one another, creating multiple connections. Using both image and text helps your audience to retain information.

You can use this to good effect in an opening statement.

Take, for instance, a case concerning a purchase contract for a residential home, promulgated by the Texas Real Estate Commission (TREC). A potential buyer puts an offer on a house. Forty-eight hours later she sends a notice of termination by email. She doesn't want to buy the house, after all. Five days after that, buyer gets a response, pointing out that seller did not pay her option fee on time, and claiming there was, therefore, no three-day option period in which seller could terminate without consequence. The responding email reads: "Your termination is rejected." At trial, seller's attorney seeks damages on the theory that buyer breached the contract by failing to close, since her termination was untimely.

In opening statement, potential buyer's attorney can tell the jury how they will hear about multiple paths to termination. That another clause permitted buyer to terminate within *seven* days of receiving Seller's Disclosure (delivered after the option contract was signed)—making the termination email timely after all. That other part of the contract permits the buyer to terminate with no other prerequisite, and for any reason.

As just words, the buyer's opening statement sounds like an unwanted short course in contract law. Or maybe it plays into the average juror's confirmation bias that lawyers play "word games" and are always "up to something."

Or buyer's counsel can use a simple graphic, like this:

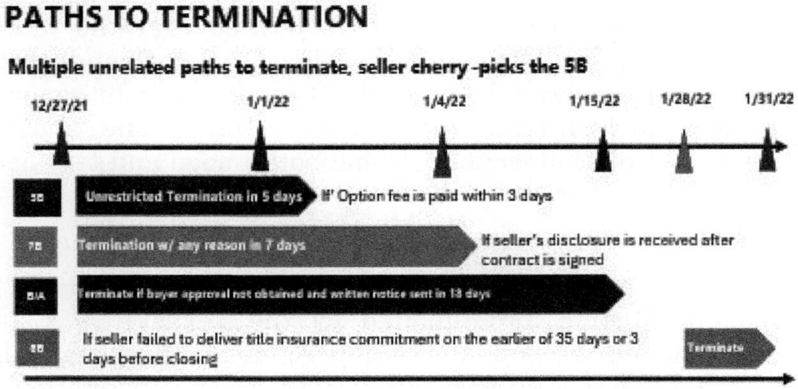


Which is easier to understand? Here the green cone represents the termination email that was timely under the second (green) path. Other cones represent later, still-timely terminations under other clauses. Easy to see, and easier to retain.

*Lesson: Show, don't just tell.*

## The Challenge: How Do I End an Opening Statement?

The close is key. A strong start is diluted with a weak ending. Of course, this is still an opening statement, so you are constrained in what you say; that is, no argument is allowed.

## Tool No. 1: Foreshadow the End

As discussed in Chapter 1 on Presentations, alerting the jury that the end is near gives them a shot of dopamine, increasing their focus and attention. Jury consultants tell lawyers that jurors hear about 30% of what is said in a courtroom. So, to make sure they pay attention to your end, say something that alerts them that your punch line is coming. Just as we did in Chapter 1 with President Lincoln's First Inaugural Address.

***By Way of Illustration:***

Any of the following does the trick:

- "I want to leave you with a final thought . . ."
- "Here is where I will close this opening . . ."
- "Finally. . . ."

Jurors will sit up and take notice.

*Lesson: Signpost the end.*

## Tool No. 2: Foreshadow the Ask

At the start of the opening, you tell the jury what brought them here today. Now you come full circle, closing the loop, telling them what you want at the end of the trial. They know you want something. Tell them.

***By Way of Illustration:***

Whether in a criminal or a civil case, put the ask in the future tense, indicating you will ask them after they have heard all the evidence. Doing otherwise is argumentative, presuming upon the jury and its role. At this stage, the lawyers have little established credibility.

Here is a suggestion for a criminal defense lawyer:

> "Members of the jury (note: stay away from the movie version of "Ladies and Gentlemen"; be aware that what you call a person can matter a great deal), the evidence will show that Lupe acted in self-defense. As we have stated, there will be evidence of a credible threat to Lupe's safety, and that Lupe's response was a reasonable response to that threat. We will ask that you find her not guilty of (charge)."

What about a civil case in which you represent a plaintiff seeking damages? Yes, you will ask for a verdict in your favor, but should you state the number of damages you seek? Opinions are divided. In his illuminating book, "David Ball on Damages", Dr. David Ball suggests that you do, but carefully, as in:

> We will show you evidence of the damages suffered by Pedro. And how much it will take to fix, help, and make

up for them. By the end of the trial, you'll see why the evidence makes this the kind of case in which I will have to come back later and ask for an amount that might sound high now but which you'll later see is the proper one for this kind of case. That amount will be $________.

Deconstructing illuminates the skill with which this is constructed. It makes use of the rule of three: "fix, help, and make up for them." Each concept compliments and reinforces the other. Each alone would be weak tea, together they form a much stronger brew. Moreover, saying "by the end of the trial", the passage is not argumentative as it projects what will be asked for and why it will be. But asking for an amount can also play into the defense frame that this is all about money.

*Lesson: Transparency creates credibility.*

## Tool No. 3: Perform a Stress Test

Finally, to ensure that your opening is not objectionable, perform a stress test by asking the following questions.

### Tell and Show

- **Am I Vouching for the Credibility of a Witness?**

When you vouch for the credibility of a witness, you turn yourself into a witness. It is no longer a fair fight. So, no "I believe you will find my client to be a believable witness." This is objectionable because you are predicting a conclusion that could be reached as well as unethical, as you are now testifying. Model Rule 3.4 (e): Fairness to Opposing Party and Counsel

- **Am I Discussing the Law in Detail?**

Yes, we know, you just spent three years in law school, took the bar exam, and are steeped in the law. You can *briefly* introduce the legal issues relevant in the case but cannot delve into discussions about legal interpretations or about applying the law to the specific facts of your case.

### ➢ Am I Using Overly Emotional Language?

Save the outrage for closing. Do not say "send them a message" or remark "this is a shakedown and is all about money."

In short, do not presume to lecture to the trier of fact.

### ➢ Am I Focusing on Facts or Conclusions?

If the first, you are good to go; if the second, you are likely making an argument which is objectionable.

### *The Spotlight*

Jules M. Epstein put together a compendium of advice, "Opening Statement v. Argument—Where Is the Line," in which he assembled advice from teachers of advocacy at various law schools. "Advocacy & Evidence, Resources, Temple University, Beasley School of Law" Here is a sampling:

**Liz Lippy:**

Rhetorical questions: I find that when an opening statement includes rhetorical questions it is often argumentative. Rhetorical questions are a tool better saved for closing argument. . .

**Abbe Smith:**

When artfully describing the defendant's inattention, it's utterly unnecessary to call him careless. By saying that word, it means you *ought* to think his conduct is careless. But the carelessness is evident to the jurors when they supply *their* powers of reason to the fact. . . Argument is when I am supplying some reasoning along with the facts.

**Adam Shlahet:**

It's important to point out that argument in opening statement is a bad idea not just because it is objectionable and improper. It is bad because it is not effective. For an argument to work, first, the trier of fact must trust that the facts are what you say they are. Second, they must consider the person making the argument to be a credible person. The problem is that during the opening statement, the advocate has not earned any credibility yet at that point, the advocate is just some lawyer trying to win a case, which naturally translates to suspicion and distrust (the opposite of credibility). So, a "hard sell" at this point in the game can actually turn off a juror and taint an otherwise compelling argument.

*Lesson: Check and double check your opening. As carpenter's say, "measure twice, cut once."*

## B. Closing Arguments

### The Challenge: How Do You Prevent Snatching Defeat from the Jaws of Victory?

A trial is an intense experience for a lawyer. Zeal for the client's cause is often an intoxicating brew. Be sure not to get carried away in closing argument as two different lawyers did, to their client's detriment, as described in the next two tools.

### Tool No. 1: It's Never About You

Keep your ego out of the close.

***By Way of Illustration:***

Imagine: It's a sexual harassment case. A vulnerable young woman, Mindy Gilster, working at a bank claims sexual harassment from the bank manager. She protests, and is retaliated against for the complaint She sues, the jury agrees with her, and awards $900,000. One problem: how her lawyer communicated with the jury in closing:

> "Mindy told you when she made her complaint . . .she feared . . . retaliation for making complaints and what effect it would have on her career. Mindy Gilster had the strength to make that complaint. . .I sure didn't. I was sexually harassed by a professor at Drake (University), but I was on my way out. I was a third-year law student, and I had been student bar president for the last year, and I was well-respected and liked by my peers. I had a great relationship with the Dean of the law school because of my role as president. . . and I refused to stand up for myself. It takes great strength

and fearlessness to make a complaint against your supervisor. . . .”

And on the lawyer went. An objection was overruled. But the appeals court set aside the verdict. Why? MR 3.4 forbids a lawyer from inserting herself into a trial like this. She becomes another witness, one not subject to cross examination. *Gilster v. Primebank,* 747 F.3d 1007 (8th Cir. 2014).

Lesson: Eliminate all “I”s.

## Tool No. 2: When in Doubt, Be Professional

So, we see in Tool No. 1 that sometimes a lawyer can’t resist the temptation of inserting themselves into the action of a trial. A cousin to No. 1 is the lawyer personalizing the closing, communicating disdain for the party and counsel opposite. The point of a closing is to help win the case, not to allow the lawyer to vent. Remember: a moment’s pleasure can lead to a lifetime of regret.

***By Way of Illustration:***

A court looks collectively at comments made to determine if they are so unprofessional as to warrant the setting aside of a verdict and the ordering of a new trial. Here is a checklist of forbidden communications potentially warranting a new trial.

***Objectionable Statement Checklist***

☑ Lawyer communicates repeatedly in closing that the defendant corporation is national, not local, or from the big city, as opposed to the rural town

☑ Lawyer communicates that the jury is the “conscience of the community”, intending to invoke a sense of community loyalty, duty and expectation

☑ Lawyer makes unsupported, irresponsible attacks on the integrity of counsel opposite

☑ Lawyer personally attacks the party opposite’s character

☑ Lawyer argues the existence of material facts that are false or without basis in the record

☑ Lawyer states that the criminal Defendant must be guilty because innocent people take the stand in their defense

***The Spotlight***

The following is taken from *Clapper v. American Realty Investors, Inc.*, 95 F.4th 309, 313 (5th Cir. 2024). The appeals court set aside a verdict of $50 million due to improper statements in a closing argument. Here's a sampling:

➢ As to Counsel Opposite

After calling counsel opposite "low class," "classless," "ruthless," and "disgusting" stating:

> "(He) defied the judge. He defied the instructions of the Judge. . . He treated us all here with disrespect. He tried to hide evidence . . .Judge had to scold him. I have never seen anything like this in the over 30 years that I have practiced in this town. Never have I seen what y'all witnessed. I am embarrassed for the profession. . . I'm embarrassed."

➢ As to Party Opposite

"Calling him a "billionaire" with a 70-foot yacht who was a "financial pimple" with a case "insulting to everybody's intelligence" and "insulting to everybody's position as a juror."

*Lesson: Let the justness of your case speak for itself.*

## The Challenge: How Do I Deliver an Effective Closing Argument?

While estimates vary, jury consultants tell lawyers that around 30% of jurors have their minds made up before closing. Dr. Ball estimates that 90% *think* they have their minds made up. In any event there is still room for the art of the closing to kick in, swaying their opinion.

## Tool No. 1: Skip the Throat Clearing

As with your opening stop all throat clearing. In opening the jury is primed at the outset to hear what your case is all about. Now in closing the jury is primed to hear what you want them to do. There is business for them to attend to.

### Tell and Show

At a closing's start, eliminate unnecessary "throat clearing." It often comes in two flavors: excessive gratitude and personal stories.

➢ Excessive gratitude

"Thank you for your service on this jury. It is a great privilege to serve, is it not? So, few countries have the jury system" and on and on.

This is closing, not a civics lesson. Get to the point.

➢ Personal stories

Lawyers here try and endear themselves to the jury. This does not work and can, in fact, be counterproductive. Here are two from trials in which Professor Maslanka participated.

➢ "Today is the first day of school and I walked my daughter to school because we need to keep what is important in mind," and on and on.

➢ "I may seem a little sleepy this morning. Well, I have a new baby, and you know how that is, but I will try to focus and help you understand the case . . ." and on and on.

*Lesson: Once more, with emphasis: the case is not about you!*

## Tool No. 2: Starting the Closing

As with opening statement, how you start is crucial. Audience attention is focused on you and what you will say.

### Tell and Show

In his book, Dr. David Ball advises that you tell the jury that they have three jobs, not one. This comes as a surprise to them, and grabs their attention, because they think there will only be one—to decide the case.

Yes, that is the first with the second being to make sure that everyone on the jury follows the law as the judge instructs. But the third—and the key one—is this:

"Before you answer any jury verdict questions, you will have to explain to each other why you feel the way you do about each question."

This is genius and leads to Tool No. 3.

*Lesson: Let jurors know that they must defend the position they take in the jury room.*

## Tool No. 3: Remind, Never Lecture

Part of your decision in closing is deciding upon your tone. As stated at the start of this book, *how* you say something is just as important as what you say.

### Tell and Show

Here is the temptation: certainty coupled with thunderous declarations. "XYZ occurred and thus you must find for my client!" But not a one of us, jurors included, want a figurative index finger pointing in our direction accompanied by a lecturing tone. Resist temptation: It is always better to remind than to lecture. Here is a pop quiz: there were two seat belt campaigns in the U.S. One failed, one succeeded. Here are their tag lines:

(a) "Buckle Up, It's the law."

(b) "Click it or Ticket."

The second tag line succeeded. Why? People were given a choice. Let jurors know they have a choice:

- "Let me suggest to you that the answer to this question is "yes". Here is why. . ."

➢ "In fixing damages, consider this as a range supported by the evidence. . ."

*Lesson: Choices are a winning communication tactic, mandates are not.*

## Tool No. 4: Empower Your Friends on the Jury

Here is a waste of time: *you* trying to convince those on the jury who are dead set against you that they should come around to your point of view. They will not.

### Tell and Show

Here is a valuable use of time: empowering those on the jury who are leaning towards your point of view to make your arguments for you. Fellow jurors are more likely to listen to them than to you.

***By Way of Illustration:***

Two Techniques are useful in this situation:

*Technique No. 1:* "If another juror says this, you say this. . ."

Professor Maslanka uses this formula:

Now when you are deliberating, a fellow juror might say, "what about XYZ point?" And that is a valid point. (You do not want to insult that juror.) If so, *remind* that juror of ABC. ("Remind" is an effective soft word that is more effective than the harsher language of, "Tell them about this evidence.")

Say ABC twice if it's important! Look at those you think are leaning towards your position or who agree with your position.

*Technique No. 2:* Use the "More Likely" Technique

Commitment that is internally developed is always more powerfully embraced than a commitment that is externally imposed. Try this in closing: Use a chart with two columns—the party opposite's version on the left, your version on the right—and ask, "What is more likely?" Then explain why it's your version. This technique taps into the power of contrast, which is a fundamental organizing principle of our brains.

*Lesson: Arm your friends on the jury. Don't try and disarm your enemies.*

## Tool No. 5: The Trifecta—Voice/Pacing/Hands

As with presentations, consider your entire body as a communication tool.

### Tell and Show

- Voice

Use your voice to underscore your points—slightly raised voice level, slightly lower voice level. Never get stuck in one gear. No one wants to listen to a humming refrigerator.

- Pacing

Use an effective pause—coupled with a rhetorical question—as we saw earlier in Chapter 1 in the John Keats ode, "To Autumn":

***Option A:***

"Where are the songs of spring? [Pause] Ay, where are they? Think not of them, thou hast thy music too."

Or

***Option B:***

"Where are the songs of Spring? Think not of them, thou hast thy music too."

*Option A* is more effective communication. The pause/question allows a listener to cognitively catch up, doesn't it? It allows them to take a mental breath. It quiets their minds and lets them absorb your message.

- Hands

No money for a fancy, high tech timeline? Create one using your hands. Each can be used as endpoints, moved closer or further apart to show spans of time, or a point in time. More on hands in the Next Tool.

*Lesson: Be all in when closing.*

## Tool No. 6: Create Powerful Images

You want people to remember what you say. Once again, use the power of the concrete to construct a lasting image.

### Tell and Show

Let's stay with imagery for a minute. Which Option is stronger in closing?

***Option A*:**

"Recall that Joe Witness testified to ABC."

Or

***Option B*:**

"Let's think back to the testimony of Joe Witness. Recall last Tuesday, when he was sitting in that witness stand" (pointing to the witness stand) and testified to ABC."

The best option is *Option B* because it is concrete and therefore more memorable.

Also consider, in addressing the jury the following options:

***Option A*:**

"Here is a key point to remember when you deliberate . . ."

Or

***Option B*:**

"(Raising you index finger) If there is one thing to remember in deliberating, here it is. . ."

That's right, *Option B.* A jury will associate the raised finger with your point. The message you are communicating will be encoded in their brains. A juror will, in deliberations, actually raise their finger and mimic you. (Watching a jury focus group do so is educational.)

*Lesson: Choreograph the closing.*

## Tool No. 7: Stress the Implausibility of the Party Opposite's Core Argument

Unlike the opening, a close should directly attack the core argument of the party opposite. One way is to argue that their core argument makes no sense.

### *The Spotlight*

Imagine it's June 1994 and you are watching the local news. Outlets start reporting about O.J. Simpson, a famous football player and now Hollywood celebrity. He is charged with murdering his former wife and her friend. You watch the lengthy trial, and hear he is acquitted. His main defense was that he was set up by the LA police.

The late Vincent Bugliosi wrote *Outrage: The Five Reasons Why O.J. Simpson Got Away with Murder*. One reason Bugliosi gave for the acquittal was that the district attorney failed to address in any meaningful way the core argument of the defense. Bugliosi sets out what he would have argued. We provide a small portion. Note how he builds his argument step by step by step, brick by brick. Note how he effectively communicates by using "you'd have to believe."

> *To believe a frame up, in addition to the many people who would have had to be involved you'd have to believe that the two teams of LAPD detectives in the case (who did not know one another)—arrive at the murder scene in the middle of the night and all suddenly agree that whoever killed these two poor people, they didn't care, they were going to let the real killer or killers go free—there were no dissents—to frame someone they believed to be innocent. . . if you plant evidence and testify falsely in a capital case. . . you can get the death penalty yourself.*

*Lesson: Now, that's a closing argument—Short, punchy, declarative.*

## Tool No. 8: Know This: You'll Win Some, You'll Lose Some

Our last piece of communication advice is not for the client, it is for you, the reader.

### Tell and Show

It is the Summer of 1981. Professor Maslanka is in a bar review course, listening to a lawyer teaching on some obscure topic on the Louisiana Bar Exam. The lawyer suddenly stops and remarks:

"Now that I have captive audience, I want to get something off my chest. It has nothing to do with the bar exam but has everything to do with your life as a lawyer. (Pause). There are cases you will win that you should lose, and, well, there are cases you should lose that you are going to win and which it turns out sometimes comes down to chance and circumstance. But what is never up to chance and circumstance is how much effort you put into your case, how much you care about your client, how much you and the client learn from your experience. That's 100% up to you."

*Lesson: You can only do what you can do.*

## WHAT SHOULD YOU DO NOW?

# PART 1

Congratulations! You have reached the end of this book—but certainly not the end of your development of the foundational skill of communication.

Your authors hope we have been mentors to you, in the best sense of the word. And that you found (or adapted) several new ideas. We encourage you to continue expanding on the ideas presented here.

And now an important question—what's next?

Early in her practice, the late leadership coach and mentor Dale Howe remarked to Professor LeBoeuf: "I will know I did my job when I see you mentor others."

It is our hope for you that you take what you learned—results of cognitive studies, best practices in working with neurodivergent colleagues and clients, techniques for gathering information from and advising clients, approaches to negotiation and persuasion—and share it with mentees of your own.

Your understanding of your new skillset is best exhibited in what you share—and in what you add to it.

Other candidates for Challenges or Tools or The Spotlight? Email us at:

Michael.Maslanka@untdallas.edu

Kelly.864@osu.edu

Nicole@leboeuflaw.com

Now, go forth and commune!

## What Should You Do Now?

# Part 2

Education is a continuing process. Here are some resources for you to review in continuing your development as an effective communicator.

***Books***


Adichie, C. N. (2006). *Half of a Yellow Sun*. Alfred A. Knopf.

Beckwith, Harry (1997). *Selling the Invisible: A Field Guide to Modern Marketing*, Warner Books.

Birkman Fink, Sharon & Capparell, Stephanie (2002). *The Birkman Method: Your Personality at Work*, Jossey-Bass.

Clark, R. H. (2005). *Addressing The Jury: Opening Statement and Closing Argument*. Thomson/West.

Clark, R. P. (2006). *Writing Tools: 55 Essentia Strategies for Every Writer (10th anniversary ed.)*. Little, Brown and Company.

Duarte, N. (2010). *Resonate: Present Visual Stories that Transform Audiences*. Wiley.

Hartman, Taylor (1999) *The Color Code*, Scribner.

Heath, C., & Heath, D. (2013). *Decisive: How to Make Better Choices in Life and Work*. Crown Business.

Hosseini, K. (2003). *The Kite Runner*. Riverhead Books.

Kahneman, D. (2011). *Thinking, Fast and Slow*. Farrar, Straus and Giroux.

Maister, David H., Green, Charles H., & Galford, Robert M. (2000), *The Trusted Advisor*, Free Press.

McMasters, A. (2022). *Listening Without Agenda: Practical Steps for Effective Listening*. Crucial Listening Press.

Moss, H. (2021). *Great minds think differently: Neurodiversity for lawyers and other professionals*. American Bar Association.

Pinker, S. (2014). *The Sense of Style: The thinking person's guide to writing in the 21st century*. Viking.

Salacuse, J. W. (2020). *The Art of Advice: How to Give and Receive Advice Effectively at Work and in Life*. Palgrave Macmillan.

Tavis, C., & Aronson, E. (2007). *Mistakes Were Made But Not by Me): Why we Justify Foolish Beliefs, Bad Decisions, and Hurtful Acts*.

Varol, O. (2023). *Awaken your Genius: Escape Conformity, Ignite creativity & Become Extraordinary*. Wiley.

### ***Journal & Magazine Articles***

Barry, P. (2018). The Rule of Three. *Legal Communication & Rhetoric: JALWD, 15*, 247–261.

Epstein, J. M. (2019). Opening Statement v. Argument—Where is the line. *The Practical Litigator, 30(3)*, 1–12.

Fisher, C. M., & Yip, J. (2025, May–June). Are You Really a Good Listener? *Harvard Business Review*.

Gallo, A. (2021, November 24). Giving Thanks at Work: An HBR guide. *Harvard Business Review*.

Goldin-Meadow, S., & Alibali, M. W. (2013). Gesture's role in speaking, learning, and creating language. *Annual Review of Psychology, 64(1)*, 257–283.

Heritage, J., & Greatbatch, D. (1986). Generating Applause: A study of rhetoric and response at party political conferences. *American Journal of Sociology, 92(1)*, 110–157.

Nawaz, S. (2018, October 17). How to Blow a Presentation to the C-suite. *Harvard Business Review*.

Scinto, J. (2014, April 15). 5 Tips for Powerful Audience Participation. *Fast Company*. https://www.fastcompany.com

Weeks, H. (2008, January). Taking the Stress out of Stressful conversations. *Harvard Business Review*.

Baile, W. F., Buckman, R., Lenzi, R., Glober, G., Beale, E. A., & Kudelka, A. P. (2000). SPIKES—A six-step protocol for delivering bad news: Application to the patient with cancer. *The Oncologist, 5(4),* 302–311.

### *Blogs & Online Resources*

Ramanathan, A. (2025, January 17). 5 steps to anticipate audience questions and prepare in advance. *WordCortex Blog.* URL: https://wordcortex.com

WordCortex. (n.d.). Show bites: Hook your audience with a cold open. *WordCortex Blog.* URL: https://wordcortex.com/

Cohen, S. (n.d.). Education by starting at their level of understanding. *Harvard Division of Continuing Education.*

Anderson, C. (2016). *TED's secret to great public speaking* [Video]. TED Conferences. URL: https://www.ted.com/talks/chris_anderson_ted_s_secret_to_great_public_speaking

Taylor, J. B. (2008). *My stroke of insight* [Video]. TED Conferences. URL: https://www.ted.com/talks/jill_bolte_taylor_my_stroke_of_insight

Borton, T. (1970). *Reach, touch, and teach.* McGraw-Hill.

Podcast: Disability 24/7. (n.d.). Listen on Spotify: https://open.spotify.com/show/2fQ2oSYc2VUHGAGo7eFOIY

Podcast: The Neurodiversity Podcast (Host: Emily Kircher-Morris). Listen on: https://neurodiversitypodcast.com/